KING ARTHUR AND THE ROUND TABLE

See p .91

They laid their spears in rest and charged

KING ARTHUR
AND
THE ROUND TABLE

by

ALICE M. HADFIELD

Illustrated with eight colour plates
and fourteen black & white drawings
by
DONALD SETON CAMMELL

LONDON: J. M. DENT & SONS LTD
NEW YORK: E. P. DUTTON & CO. INC.

The references to Arthur, King of Britain, go back before the Middle Ages, before Norman times, before Norsemen and Anglo-Saxon, before Alfred and the welding into one kingdom of Saxons, Danes, and Britons, back into the Dark Ages between that welding and the first earliest unity under the Romans. The history of King Arthur is almost the only constant and recurring theme among the confused tales of the centuries between the departure of the Romans and a return of Christianity to the Anglo-Saxon kingdoms in the seventh century.

Men said that Arthur did not die, and certainly thoughts of him did not die in their minds. Century after century historians and poets wrote his story again, and each one suited his writing to his own times. The story of Arthur crossed the seas, and travelled all the roads of medieval Europe, and returned in the books of French historians and poets. But to English people the most fresh and real telling of it is in the book 'Morte d'Arthur,' or 'Death of Arthur,' by Sir Thomas Malory, who combined the French poems he had read with stories about King Arthur still told in Wales.

He wrote of King Arthur with his thoughts on his own century, the fifteenth. In his pages we find, not leather-clad, sword- and axe-armed Britons as they probably were under King Arthur in the sixth century, but English knights in iron armour, with the lance and shield and horse of the Wars of the Roses. He writes of a vivid and violent age. Knights weep and kiss and pray as readily as they strike and kill. It is a world of men, and the world of women is only glimpsed through the famous names of Guenevere and Dindrane. It is a religious world, where Jesus Christ is ever present to the minds of these knights, and His service is as clear and real as that of the King, a world where every one moves naturally in and out of church, and where mercy, forgiveness, and generosity with money are part of a knight's daily duty. But whatever century we are reading of, the meaning behind the story of Arthur shines through and speaks to our own minds in our own age.

 Made in Great Britain at the Aldine Press, Letchworth, Herts, for J. M. Dent & Sons Ltd, Aldine House, Albemarle Street, London. First published in this edition 1953. Last reprinted 1975.

ISBN: 0 460 05023 0

CONTENTS

SOURCES

The Works of Sir Thomas Malory: edited by Eugene Vinaver. 3 vols. Clarendon Press, 1947.

The Mabinogion: translated by Thomas and Gwyn Jones. Everyman's Library No. 97.

The writings of *Wace*: the Norman poet of the twelfth century, and those of *Layamon*: the Worcestershire priest and poet, also of the twelfth century, are both to be found in *Arthurian Chronicles.* Everyman's Library No. 447.

The High History of the Holy Grail: Everyman's Library, No. 445.

The poetry quotations are from Tennyson's *Idylls of the King.*

ILLUSTRATIONS

Colour

Black and White

THE COMING OF MERLIN

IT was Merlin the wizard who caused Arthur to be King of Britain. No one else knew that Arthur was a prince, and that he had been entrusted to Merlin to be watched over in secret and brought to the throne.

Merlin's own origin is as hidden as Arthur's. Old even when Arthur was young, the wizard's boyhood reaches far back into the years of warfare, before Arthur brought peace to Britain. Before Arthur was king, his father Uther reigned, and before Uther came Aurelius, and before Aurelius came Vortiger, and it is during the reign of Vortiger that Merlin first appears, aged nine years old.

In Merlin's youth the island of England, Scotland, and Wales was called by two names—Logres or Britain. The Romans had called it Britain from the name of a tribe of people living in it, but Logres was the name that its own people used. From the beginning it was an island of marvels, with its mysterious temple of Stonehenge, its white-robed Druid priests, its gold, and its pearls. The stormy seas which beat around its coasts prevented sailors or traders from easily reaching the island, and added to its mystery.

In the first century after the birth of Christ the Romans conquered Britain, and added it to their empire. They brought peace to the island, built roads and towns, and taught the people how to obey the laws and live peaceably together, instead of continually fighting each other. Among the Roman soldiers were some who had been told about Jesus Christ and His teaching. They spread the news to people in Britain. So the foundations of the Kingdom of Britain were laid in Christianity and law.

Four hundred years went by. Britain prospered, but Rome weakened. Her armies had to be drawn back nearer to Rome itself, and by A.D. 410 the last of the legions had left the conquered island. By this time a great many of the British people were Christian. They had built churches, and decorated them with beautiful work in gold, silver, and woven hangings. Tales of these riches had reached the people living along the coasts of western Europe, where nobody was Christian. They were 'heathen men,' brave but savage and greedy, and they worshipped gods who they believed demanded that men should fight and kill each other. These 'old gods' as they were called particularly ordered their worshippers to kill the followers of Jesus Christ, because He taught quite a different way of life. This belief, combined with their greed for the beautiful things in the Christian churches, urged them to begin to raid the coasts of Britain as soon as the strong Roman troops defending the shores were gone. Success drew more and more raiders, and the ending of winter storms was the signal for heathen bands to be on the move all over Denmark and North Germany, to cross the narrow seas, and to burn and rob the villages of eastern and southern Britain.

So came dark days for Britain. Churches were robbed, and priests and people killed or taken as slaves. British chiefs would try to resist, but often they were traitors who made peace with the invaders in order themselves to oppress the people. Men spoke of the days when Britain was peaceful and united under one rule, and they longed for a good king who would bring back peace, order, and justice. Even Christianity was in danger, for few priests or hermits were left to teach the people, and the heathen invaders forced them by threat of torture and death to worship their own savage gods.

At last one British lord named Constantine succeeded in setting up a little kingdom of Christian peace and order in the south-west. People believed that he was the king they sought and longed for, the rightful holder of the Dragonship or Kingdom of Britain. He had three sons: Constance, Aurelius, and Uther. But when he died a Welsh lord named Vortiger arranged the murder of young Constance, the heir, and when Constantine's widow fled from Britain with the two younger boys, Aurelius and Uther, Vortiger seized power and made himself King of Britain.

Vortiger was one of those lords who made friends with the Saxons whom he invited to his kingdom, but he was soon to know the treachery of the heathen invaders. One of his old allies, the Saxon Hengist, came into south Britain with a great host, and a feast was held at Stonehenge. The British lords sat down unarmed, thinking all were friends. But the Saxons hid daggers under their cloaks, and at a signal from Hengist they fell upon the British while a toast was being drunk, and slew almost every man. Vortiger himself was taken prisoner, and to save his life he basely gave away his lands, towns, and villages to the Saxon enemy, instead of defending them to the death.

Then Vortiger escaped from the enemy camp. He fled westwards over the Severn to his own land of Wales, snatching what sleep he could by day, and riding and running by night, until in a cave of the Welsh mountains he was safe at last. There the British began to gather round him to resist the hated Saxons who were slaying and burning all over southern Britain.

The first need was for a castle, so as to make a centre of resistance for the countryside, for the invading armies had no heavy engines with which to batter down strong walls. A wise man advised Vortiger to build his castle on the mount of Reir, and so he went there with his followers.

First they dug a mighty moat or dike all round the site, sounding horns to summon men from mountain and valley to come to their aid. Working with desperate haste they dug, cut down trees, measured and marked out, mixed lime and collected stones, and finally were ready to begin to build the wall above the dike. But they could get no further. Each day part of the great wall was built; each night it fell to the ground. In the morning they raised it once more, in the night again the stones fell, yet no man had harmed the wall. Thus they laboured for a week, and grew more and more afraid as news came of the hosts of Hengist raging nearer.

Then Vortiger sent for all the Welsh wizards and wise men, and commanded them to tell him why the wall fell when no man had laid hands on it. For three nights under the moon the wizards practised their arts, some in the darkness of the forests, others at the cross-roads among the echoes of the mountains. But neither from tree nor stone came an answer. Only one wizard, Joram by name, uttered a strange saying. He pronounced that if there could be found a boy who had no father, and if his heart's blood were taken and mingled with the lime of the wall, then it would stand until the end of time.

The saying was strange and mysterious but the King obeyed it. He sent messengers all over Wales to search for a boy who had no father. Two of the messengers went due west, where now Carmarthen lies, and outside the town wall they found a broad meadow where the children played. The King's men were tired and saddened by their hopeless quest, and they sat down in the shade of a tree to rest, idly watching the boys at their play. Near them a

For three nights under the moon the wizards practised their arts

quarrel sprang up, and two boys had a fight, one soon getting the better of the other. The lad who had been beaten made off, shouting taunts as he ran: 'I 'll pay you out for this, nobody's son! I am the son of a chief. *You* ought to be a slave! Who is your father? You never had one!' And the boys who had gathered round to see the fight began to set upon the lad.

The King's men, startled by the cries of 'Nobody's son,' dragged the struggling boys apart, and asked what the uproar was all about. They were told that the boy's name was Merlin. He was a slim, strong boy of about nine years old, with black hair and light grey eyes. The men took him to one of the elders in the town, Eli, who said that it was true that Merlin was said to have no father, and that his mother had become a nun. When the King's messengers had explained their business Eli brought the mother and her son to the King's mountain stronghold.

The mother told Vortiger that she was the daughter of a Welsh chieftain, Conaan, well known in these mountains. When she was fifteen she began to fall into trances and to see strange visions, and in these she came to know a tall knight clad in gold. Time after time he came to her. She knew neither his name nor where he came from, whether of God or the devil. Then he ceased to come, and the dreams and visions ceased also. Afterwards the boy Merlin was born.

'Alas, as I pray for mercy, I know not any more to say of my son, how he came into the world.'

Magan, one of the King's councillors, who understood the journeyings of the stars and the mysteries of the sky, told the King that the gold-clad knight was one of the creatures who live in the sky, neither angels nor men. They are mischievous creatures, he said, and love to play

See p. 26

When they reached it, Arthur took the sword by the hilt

tricks on people. One had taken the form of a handsome knight and deceived the daughter of Conaan.

Now Merlin wanted to know why all his history was being thus traced out. So the King told him the story of the falling of the wall, and of the strange saying of Joram, that would mean the boy's death.

Merlin stood and looked slowly round the group of magicians kneeling or standing before the King in their magic robes and horned head-dresses. He looked at the ring of warriors with their spears who guarded every way, and he was not afraid. He threw up his head and spoke out to the King.

'Your wise men deceive you,' he cried. 'They tell you lies. Joram is my enemy, but let him and his companions come before you and I will tell you the truth about the wall and prove to you that they are lying. If I make the wall stand, give me their heads!'

The challenge was taken up. The King stood on the top of the dike bank with Joram and the magicians, and with the leaders of his army. There also stood the boy Merlin. Beside them lay the broken stones of the wall, and around rose the great mountains.

Then Merlin cried: 'Tell me, Joram, traitor! Why does the wall fall? What shall men find at the bottom of the wall?'

Joram did not know.

'King, keep your promise!' Merlin cried again. 'Order the dike to be dug seven feet deeper. You will find a stone, well cut and broad.'

They dug and found the stone.

Merlin cried again: 'King, keep your promise! Tell me, Joram, man to me most hateful, what kind of thing is under this stone?'

Joram was silent—he could not tell.

So Merlin answered for him. 'There is water under here. Take away the stone, and you will find water.'

And they did so, and again he challenged Joram, demanding that he should tell them what lived at the bottom of the water, winter and summer. Still Joram did not know.

Merlin spoke. 'King, keep your promise! Have the waters drained. Below live two strong dragons, one on the north side and the other on the south. One is milk-white and the other blood-red, boldest of all dragons. At midnight they begin to fight, and the earth sinks, and so your wall totters and falls, and this is not because you need my blood for the building.'

All happened as Merlin foretold. When the dike was drained out came two dragons, white and red. They sprang on each other and fought, but neither could kill the other. At last both dragons retreated into their holes and went under the earth and were never seen again.

The King turned to Joram and his seven magicians, and ordered their heads to be cut off, so Merlin had his way. Truth and prophecy were Merlin's lifeblood indeed, and with his aid the wall was built, so that in one sense Joram spoke more truly than he knew.

Merlin now became the King's adviser. He warned him that evils were to come upon him from the sons of Constantine because of his wicked deeds. Soon, said Merlin, Aurelius and young Uther would land in Britain, in far-off Devon at Totnes, with seven hundred ships. Fly as he might Vortiger would never escape them. First Aurelius would be acclaimed as Pendragon, but he would be slain by poison. Then Uther would be Pendragon and wage great wars to bring peace at last to Britain.

Then Merlin made his great prophecy.

'Uther shall have an heir, Arthur. Out of Cornwall

shall he come, that shall be a wild boar, bristled with steel. The boar shall consume the heathen camps, he shall devour all traitors with authority, he shall kill all your rich kindred. He shall be the bravest man alive and the most noble in thought. All his foes he shall strike to the ground. I have told you the truth, but it is not easier because it is true. Fly as you may with your host, your enemies will track you down even to your own camp.'

It all happened as Merlin had foreseen. Aurelius and Uther landed and pursued Vortiger, who took refuge in a castle near the River Wye. The princes besieged him, filled the dike with branches of trees, set fire to them, and burned down the castle and Vortiger with it. Aurelius became the rightful king, and Uther followed him, while Merlin was counsellor to them both.

Thus Merlin's destiny began to fulfil itself in the coming of Arthur—the wild boar bristled with steel.

I

THE FOUNDING OF THE ROUND TABLE

CHAPTER I

THE BIRTH OF ARTHUR

THE secret of the birth of Arthur, King of Britain, is hidden from us like the secret of his end. Although he was, as Merlin prophesied, heir to Uther, no one can prove his parentage or his birth. He first comes upon the scene as a lad in his teens, living in a noble house of which he was not a son.

Those who claim that he was a man like other men tell the story thus.

When Uther was Pendragon he engaged in continuous wars with the heathen invaders. One of his own subjects fought against him as well, the Duke of Cornwall. Uther sent messages to the Duke asking him to come to his court and make peace. He came, and brought his wife Igraine with him, who was both beautiful and wise. The King and the Duke made peace. There were feasts and sports and merrymaking, and the King, who was not married, fell in love with Igraine.

As soon as she realized this she said to the Duke: 'Husband, I counsel you that we go away from here at once, and ride all night to our own castle.' They did so, and the King prepared to make war on them again.

The Duke of Cornwall manned his two chief castles, and sent Igraine to the one called Tintagel, while he himself defended Terrabil, which was famous for its secret doors and posterns in and out. Uther came with a great host and laid siege to Terrabil. But he could make no headway, and for anger and love of Igraine he fell sick. Then Sir

Ulfius, a knight of his company, went to ask Merlin for help in curing him.

He met the wizard dressed as a beggar on the road.

Merlin told him that he would cause the King to have all that he wished if in return he would perform a wish of Merlin's.

When they returned to court and told the King this, the King swore on the four Gospels to do as Merlin told him. Merlin then said that when he married Igraine he would have a child, and he must give it to Merlin to bring up. He promised that it should be for the good of the child. Uther agreed to this, and Merlin then told him what to do to win Igraine.

That day the King made a very obvious withdrawal from the siege of Terrabil, leaving some of his army encamped there, and rode towards Tintagel. The Duke's spies told him of the King's departure, and the same night he led an attacking party out of one of the postern gates, and in the fighting the Duke himself was killed. The news was brought next day to the King outside Igraine's castle at Tintagel. Then all the barons asked him to make peace with the Lady Igraine. The King asked Sir Ulfius to take messages of goodwill to her, and at last Sir Ulfius persuaded Igraine to meet the King. He then urged that they should marry. 'Our King is a strong knight and wifeless,' he said, 'and my Lady Igraine is a fair lady; it would be great joy to us all if it might please the King to make her his queen.' They were married next morning.

In time a son was born to them. Merlin came to Uther and reminded him of his promise. Heavy-hearted, the King kept his word. Then Merlin said: 'I know a lord of yours who is a very true man, and faithful, and he shall have the nourishing of your child, and his name is Sir

Ector. Let the child be delivered to me at yonder private postern, unchristened.'

The King ordered two knights and two ladies to take the child wrapped in a cloth of gold to the postern gate and give him to an unknown poor man who would be waiting. This was Merlin in disguise. He took the child, and what he did then no one knows, but in time he brought him to Sir Ector and there summoned a priest and had the child baptized and named Arthur.

Two years after this the King fell ill. Merlin summoned all the lords, and said in a loud voice: 'Sir, shall your son Arthur be King after your days of this realm with all its belongings?'

The King answered: 'I give him God's blessing and mine, and bid him pray for my soul, and tell him that he must claim the crown or lose my blessing.' Then he died, and no one knew who was the son Arthur or where he was, except Merlin, who kept silence.

Arthur was only two years old. Evil times came on Britain,

> For many a petty king ere Arthur came
> Ruled in this isle, and ever waging war
> Each upon other, wasted all the land;
> And still from time to time the heathen host
> Swarm'd overseas, and harried what was left.
> And so there grew great tracts of wilderness,
> Wherein the beast was ever more and more,
> But man was less and less till Arthur came.

That is the story of those who say that Arthur was a man born like other men.

Another story was told by Morgause Bellicent, Queen of Orkney, wife of King Lot. She was the daughter of Igraine and the Duke of Cornwall, and so by one story half-sister to King Arthur. She said that Merlin learned his magic from an old wizard named Bleys, whom he far surpassed in power but who nevertheless was his first master. Merlin became a famous wizard and Bleys was forgotten. Arthur grew up and claimed his throne, and fierce quarrelling broke out as to whether he was the rightful king or not. A message came to the Queen of Orkney from the ancient Bleys, whom every one had thought to be dead years ago. He asked her to come and hear what he must say before he died.

So the dark-eyed queen, herself a practiser of spells and magic, made her way alone along the rocky coast of her wild isle of Orkney. Holding her cloak round her in the shrieking wind, she came to the entrance of a cave in the bare cliff, and, stooping, she went in. There on the ground lay Merlin's master, shrunk to the size of a monkey by extreme old age. She seated herself beside him, and to the accompaniment of the roaring of the sea and the cries of sea-birds he told her this story.

Bleys and Merlin had been with King Uther on the night that he died. The King was childless and it was the greatest sorrow of his life. He knew that every lord would try to seize the throne, and that Britain would be torn in pieces by them. But there was no help for it and he died. The two magicians stayed awhile by his body, letting no one come in, or know that he was dead. It was night, and wind and rain were driving past the castle, and the sky was black.

They went out by a secret way from the King's room to a postern gate on the cliff above steps which led down to a cove. Wild though the night was, it was refreshing after the death-chamber. They tried to see the stars, but in the blackness could not distinguish the sea from the sky. As they came out on to the steps, suddenly in the dark there shone a ship, so high that they did not know if it was

She seated herself beside him

reared up on a monstrous wave or hung low among the stars of the sky, a ship shaped like a winged dragon and outlined in fire. Along the decks were throngs of shining figures, but before the magicians could speak the vision vanished. They hurried down to the cove and stood listening to the crash of the breakers, and watched them come roaring in, their crests gleaming with phosphorescence. Eight huge waves rolled in, each one bigger than the last,

> Till last, a ninth one, gathering half the deep
> And full of voices, slowly rose and plunged
> Roaring, and all the wave was in a flame:
> And down the wave and in the flame was borne
> A naked babe, and rode to Merlin's feet,
> Who stoopt and caught the babe, and cried 'The King!
> Here is an heir for Uther!' And the fringe
> Of that great breaker, sweeping up the strand,
> Lash'd at the wizard as he spake the word,
> And all at once all round him rose in fire,
> So that the child and he were clothed in fire.

This child, said the dying Bleys, was the Arthur about whom every one was disputing, and until the ancient man had told the Queen this truth he could not die in peace. On saying this he drew his last breath and died.

The Queen went home, and when she saw Merlin next she asked him if this story was true. But Merlin always answered questions by riddles, and he perplexed the Queen by neither confirming nor denying her story. He made a song of Arthur the new king, which ended,

> Sun, rain and sun! and where is he who knows?
> From the great deep to the great deep he goes.

CHAPTER 2

THE SWORD IN THE STONE

AFTER the death of Uther Pendragon there was no true king in Britain, because no one but Merlin knew if Arthur really existed, or where he was. The lords fought each other and each tried to make himself king. They built castles in which they themselves were safe, but from which they rode out to harry the countryside, to rob farmers and any one who had any wealth, and torture those who would not say where their wealth was hidden. Great was the misery of Britain, and cries went up for a true king who would put down the lords, protect the poor, and maintain the right for each man.

When Merlin the wizard knew that the time had come, he went to the Archbishop of Canterbury and said that if he would call the leading men to London at Christmas time, Christ, who was King of all mankind, would show some miracle at the season of His birthday to prove who was the rightful king of Britain. So the Archbishop summoned all the chief men of the kingdom to London at Christmas.

On Christmas Day they went to church. When they came out they found in the churchyard outside the east end of the church a square marble stone, in the middle of which was an anvil, and into the anvil was thrust a sword. The stone gripped the naked sword by the point, and on the blade was written in gold letters: 'Whoso pulleth out this sword of this stone and anvil, is rightwise born King of all Logres.' Here was the miracle foretold by Merlin.

Each lord tried to pull it out and all failed. Nobody could move it. The Archbishop said: 'He is not here that shall achieve this sword, but doubt not that God will make him known.'

News of the miracle was hurriedly told to all knights, with an invitation to each to try to pull out the sword. A tournament was announced for New Year's Day, after which the knights were to make the attempt.

All the great lords met again on New Year's Day. Among them was Sir Ector, who brought his son Sir Kay who had been made a knight at the previous Hallowe'en. With them rode his younger brother Arthur, who was only fifteen years old and not a knight and had no importance at all. Nor was he really Kay's brother, though no one but Sir Ector and Merlin knew this. He did not know it himself, but thought he was just Kay's younger brother.

After the church service they all rode in a gay company to the tournament field. Sir Kay suddenly realized that he had left his sword behind in his lodgings. There was no time for him to go back, for he was due to take part in the young knights' tournament, so he asked Arthur to go back for him. Arthur went as fast as he could to their lodgings. But every one had gone to see the fighting, and the house was locked. Arthur was angry and said: 'I will ride to the churchyard and take the sword with me that sticketh in the stone, for my brother shall not be without a sword this day.'

He found no one at the churchyard, for every one had gone to see the tournament. So he took the sword by the hilt and gave it a light, fierce pull, and out it came. He ran off, jumped on to his horse, and rode to the tournament field and gave Kay the sword.

Now Kay, being a knight, had been told about the

meaning of the sword in the stone. He recognized it at once. He unwisely thought he could deceive the sword, and went to his father and said: 'Sir, look, here is the sword of the stone, and so *I* must be king of this land.'

Sir Ector was amazed. But he was a wise man, and he immediately took Kay and Arthur and left the field and went back to the church. He gave Kay a Bible and told him to swear on it how he came by the sword.

Kay was frightened now, and he said: 'Sir, by my brother Arthur, for he brought it to me.'

Sir Ector looked at young Arthur, and remembered how strangely Merlin had brought him in secret as a new-born baby and told him that he was to bring him up as his own son, and that in the right time God would reveal who the child truly was.

'How did you get the sword?' said Sir Ector slowly to Arthur, standing by the altar in the quiet church.

Arthur told him exactly what he had done.

'Now,' said Sir Ector to Arthur, 'I understand you must be king of this land.'

'I?' said Arthur, astonished. 'How can that be?'

'Sir,' said Sir Ector, using the title for the first time, 'because God will have it so, for no man could have pulled out this sword unless he was the rightful king of this land. Now let me see whether you can put the sword back as it was, and pull it out again.'

'That is quite easy,' said Arthur, and they all went outside into the frosty churchyard. There stood the white stone with the anvil wedged in the top. But in the anvil there was no sword. Arthur went up to it and thrust the sword back into its slit, which gripped the blade hard.

Sir Ector tried to pull it out, to see that there was no trick. He could not move it at all. 'Now you try,' said Sir Ector to Sir Kay, and Sir Kay pulled with all his might but could not move it. 'Now you shall try,' Sir Ector said to Arthur.

'Very well,' said Arthur, and pulled it out easily.

Sir Ector and Sir Kay knelt down before Arthur.

'My own dear father and brother,' said the boy. 'Why do you kneel to me?'

Then Sir Ector told him that he was not his own son, but that Merlin had brought him as a baby to be brought up as his son in his household. 'Sir,' said Sir Ector again, 'I will ask no more of you, but that you will make my son, your foster-brother Sir Kay, steward in charge of your lands.'

Arthur answered: 'That shall be done, and no other man shall have the office while he and I live.'

Then they went to the Archbishop and told him what had happened. At the end of the New Year tournament, on the Epiphany, 6th January, all the knights tried the sword and none could move it. Then Arthur, who was not even a knight, drew it out. But the lords were angry, and refused to have a boy of fifteen, of unknown parents, as king over them. They resisted so strongly that it was not until the summer feast of Pentecost, or Whitsun, that Arthur was acknowledged the true king.

It was decided at last. Arthur took the sword in both hands and laid it on the altar where the Archbishop was standing. Then he knelt down, and the best knight present was chosen to come forward and make him knight. After that the Archbishop set on his head the crown of Britain, and, wearing it, he swore the king's oath to give justice to all men, high and low, all the days of his life. The people threw up their caps and shouted because a true king had come at last to punish the oppressors and to defend the poor.

But many of the great lords were not pleased. The

King took away their posts from those who were not to be trusted, and made young Sir Kay Steward and Seneschal of Logres, Sir Baudwin Constable, Sir Ulfius Chamberlain, and Sir Brastias Warden of the North, where many enemies lay waiting in strength to resist the King. Arthur knew that a peaceful reign did not lie ahead of him. There were fierce raiders from over the seas, and hostile British lords in strong castles, and even treacherous men among his own advisers. The strongest lord might have felt that a heavy task lay before him in ruling the kingdom rightly, or even in keeping his throne at all. This lad of fifteen faced it bravely, knowing that God had called him to it, and therefore he could do it.

CHAPTER 3

THE SWORD IN THE LAKE

A FEW weeks after Arthur had been made king he was out riding one morning early. He carried only a light sword, and not the one which he had pulled from the stone. That sword still lay on the altar where he had placed it at his coronation. As he rode down a woodland path he came on the wizard Merlin being attacked by three men. When they saw an armed knight on horseback bearing down on them they ran away.

'Oh, Merlin,' said Arthur, 'if I had not been here you would have been killed in spite of all your crafts.'

'No,' said Merlin, 'I should not, for I could have saved myself if I had wanted to. You are more near death than I am, for you are going towards death unless God is your friend.'

As they went on, the track led to a fountain. Blocking the way was an armed knight sitting in a chair. He refused to let them pass without fighting him, and said it was his custom. 'Any one who does not like my custom can alter it if he can.'

'I will alter it,' said Arthur. So the knight got on to his horse and they took their spears and charged each other. Each spear shattered in splinters on each shield. They leaped off their horses and fell upon each other with their swords. The blows rang on their armour and ripped great gashes through the leather joints so that the blood ran out. As they strove to and fro the trampled ground was stained with blood. At last King Arthur smote such a blow that his sword was broken in two. The knight cried out that he was in his power and must yield as beaten or be killed.

'As for death,' said King Arthur, 'welcome be it when it comes, and I would rather die than yield to you as beaten,' and he sprang on to the knight and took him by the middle and threw him down. But the knight was a much heavier man than Arthur and he wrestled so fiercely that he got Arthur down under him and held him helpless. As his dagger was raised to kill him Merlin cast a spell over him and he fell to the earth in a deep sleep. Merlin helped Arthur up and mounted the knight's horse, and they rode away to have Arthur's wounds dressed. The King was angry because he thought Merlin had beaten the knight by a spell, and he had been a good fighter and had fought fairly and bravely.

'I told you what a knight he was,' answered Merlin. 'You would have been killed if I had not been there. There is no mightier knight than he, and after this he shall do you good service. His name is Pellinore, and he shall have two sons whose names will be Percivale of Wales and Lamorak of Wales. He will tell you the name of the son of your own sister that shall be the destruction of all this kingdom.'

This was an evil prophecy, but Arthur was too young to be disturbed over a child who was not yet born. As they rode, the King said: 'I have no sword.'

'Never mind,' answered Merlin, 'near here is a sword that shall be yours if I have any skill.'

So they rode till they came to a lake, in the middle of which Arthur saw a sight as strange as the marble stone and anvil in the churchyard. Rising out of the water was an arm, clothed in soft white silk, or samite, holding a sword in its hand.

'Look,' said Merlin, 'there is that sword I spoke of.'

As they gazed, they saw a boat moving across the water with a damsel in it.

'That is the Lady of the Lake,' said Merlin, 'and under

that lake is a rock, inside which is as fair a place as any on earth, and richly kept. This damsel is coming to you, so speak well to her and she will give you the sword.'

The boat drew to land, and the lady greeted Arthur, who returned her greeting. 'Damsel,' he said, 'what sword is that, which yonder arm holds above the water? I wish it were mine, for I have no sword.'

'Sir Arthur, King,' she answered, 'that sword is mine, and if you will give me a gift when I ask it, you shall have it.'

Arthur knew that Merlin would have warned him if the lady were an enemy, so he replied: 'By my faith, I will give you whatever gift you shall ask.'

'Very well,' she said. 'Get into the boat and row to the sword, and take it and the scabbard with you, and I will ask my gift when I see my time.'

So Arthur and Merlin got off their horses and tied them to two trees, and went into the boat. They rowed across the lake to the mysterious arm, and when they reached it Arthur took the sword by the hilt and the hand let go and the arm withdrew under the still water. They did not pause there, but rowed straight back to the shore. The Lady of the Lake had disappeared. The King sprang out of the boat and, once safely on shore, examined the sword and saw how magnificent it was. Its name was on it, carved into the blade, 'Excalibur,' and below it on one side, 'Take me,' and on the other, 'Cast me away.'

Then they took their horses again and rode back to the court in Caerleon.

Arthur's friends among the knights were very thankful to see him, for no one had known what had happened to him. He told them all his adventures, and they were amazed that he should so risk his life single-handed. But all the true knights said it was merry to serve under such a leader who would put himself in danger like any ordinary knight.

CHAPTER 4

SIR BALIN AND SIR BALAN

KING ARTHUR was now established as King of Britain. But in fact his law was obeyed only in a small part of his kingdom, because heathen lords from across the sea were in possession of most of it. He had two chief cities, Caerleon on the Usk in Wales, and Camelot in the centre of southern England. A smaller town was Carbonek, on the sea coast of South Wales. From these centres Arthur and his knights began to wage war on the heathen, attacking them continually and giving them no peace. Slowly they drove them further and further to the north and east, and slowly more and more of the kingdom was won back to order and to Christ.

During one of these wars in the north of England, a cousin of the King had been killed by a knight of the north country named Balin. Instead of killing him in revenge for his cousin the King took him back to his court as a prisoner, to learn the ways of knighthood and his own good laws. For some months Balin lived at court, a stranger speaking with a strange north-country accent, pining for the grey mountains and rough speech of Northumberland. He was treated with respect for his huge height and strength of arm, as well as for his fierce brooding temper, but he remained a prisoner and a stranger.

While the court was at London, Rience, lord of North Wales under King Arthur, seized the chance to break into England across the rich valleys of Shropshire and carry off people and cattle. So King Arthur made ready to march against him. One day, during the preparations, a damsel came before the King wearing a heavy sword which she could hardly carry. She said that she could only be relieved of the sword by a knight who was a good man in arms and free from villainy, treachery, and treason. All the knights tried to draw the sword, but all failed.

Balin stood at the back, an uncouth figure who had never outgrown his name of Balin the Savage. His eyes were fixed on the damsel and his heart beat heavily with a sudden knowledge of his fate. He waited till she left the court after the failure of all the knights, and then he followed her.

He spoke awkwardly: 'Damsel, I pray you of your courtesy, let me try as well as these lords; although I am poorly dressed, in my heart I am as good as some of these others and something tells me I shall succeed. Manhood and worth is hid within man's person, and many a worthy knight is not known to everybody.'

So she let him try, and as soon as he laid his hand on the pommel the sword came lightly out in his hand. Balin stood staring at it, a fierce exultation in his heart. He, the stranger, the prisoner, he had done it, he had been more worthy than them all.

The court was stirred with excitement, and many of the lesser knights were annoyed. The lady asked Balin for the sword back again.

He glared at her. 'Nay,' he answered, 'this sword will I keep, unless it is taken from me by force.'

'You are not wise,' said the damsel, 'to keep the sword from me, for you shall kill with it the best friend you have and the man you love best in the world, and the sword shall be your destruction.'

Now the man that Balin loved best in the world was

Balan his brother, up in the rocky village in Northumberland. He was so sure that he could never attack his brother that he took no notice of the warning, and repeated that no one should take the sword away from him.

So the lady departed, and as after this proof of his honour, Balin could no longer be held prisoner he made ready to depart too, his heart already eating up the miles between him and his northern country. But suddenly into the court there came a strange woman, very magnificently dressed. It was the Lady of the Lake, who had given the King his sword Excalibur out of the lake, and had been promised any gift which she chose to ask whenever she should claim it. She challenged the King and demanded her gift. He told her to speak on.

'I ask the head of the knight that won the sword, or else the head of the damsel who brought it; for he slew my brother, and that gentlewoman was the cause of my father's death.'

'Truly,' said King Arthur, 'I may not with honour grant either of their heads. Ask anything else and I will give it to you.'

'I ask nothing else,' said the lady. But as she spoke Balin burst through the ranks of the knights, carrying his new sword drawn in his hand, and his temper blazing in his eyes. He strode to the lady and cried: 'Evil be upon you! You would have my head, and so you shall lose yours,' and in front of the King he cut off her head at one sweep of the sword.

The King sprang up. 'What have you done?' he cried. 'You have shamed me and all my court, for this was a lady to whom I was indebted, and she came here under my safe conduct. I shall never forgive you. Leave the court as quickly as you can.'

So Balin the Savage left the court, half glad to be going

home and half sorry he had to leave in disgrace. Suddenly he decided to win back the approval of the King by attacking the rebel lord Rience and if possible killing him in combat. He gave the head of the Lady of the Lake to his squire and told him to ride with it to Northumberland, while he himself struck across England to the west.

An Irish knight of King Arthur's court called Lanceor rode after him and challenged him to a battle because of the disgrace he had brought on the court by killing a woman there. Balin accepted the challenge very readily. They fought, and Balin killed Lanceor. While he was taking off his helm and breathing hard after the fight, a damsel came riding fast on a light horse. When she saw Lanceor dead she burst into a great cry, for he was her lover, and said: 'Oh, Balin, two bodies thou hast slain and one heart, and two hearts in one body, and two souls thou hast lost.' And before Balin could stop her she seized Lanceor's sword and killed herself with it. Balin was horrified, for this was the second woman whose death he had caused.

Not knowing what to do he looked round him in distress, and saw a knight coming out of the edge of the wood. He looked at his armour and the picture on his shield and his heart leaped, for it was his brother Balan. They rode to each other and kissed together and wept for joy.

Balin told him all his doings, and this last tragedy.

'It is a great pity,' said Balan, 'but you must take the adventures God appoints you.'

This cheered Balin, but he answered: 'Truly I am very sorry that my Lord Arthur is displeased with me, for he is the best knight that reigns now on earth, and I am determined to get back into his good pleasure or else my life is worth nothing.' He told Balan of his plan to attack Sir Rience, and they rode off together towards the west.

On the way they met with the wizard Merlin, who told

Balin that he had buried Sir Lanceor in a meadow at Camelot and made a monument over him. He warned Balin that he had brought trouble on himself by the death of Lanceor's damsel.

Balin protested: 'I could not save her. She killed herself suddenly.'

'I am very sorry,' Merlin repeated. 'Because of the death of that lady you will strike a blow which will be the most dolorous that was ever struck except the one which pierced our Lord, for you will hurt the truest knight and the man of most worth who is now living, and through that stroke three kingdoms shall be in poverty, misery, and wretchedness for twelve years, and the knight will not be healed of that wound for many years.'

At this Balin grew angry. 'If I thought you were telling the truth that I should do such a thing as that I would kill myself to prove you a liar,' he said. But when Merlin offered his wizard's help to find Rience and attack him the brothers were pacified.

'Come now,' said Merlin, 'you shall have great honour, and see that you do all in a knightly manner, for you will have need of it.'

'As for that,' said Balin, 'do not worry, we will do all we can.'

Then Merlin led them to some thick trees by the grass highway. It was already dark. Almost at once they heard the sound of horses' hoofs muffled on the turf, the clink of bits, and creak of armour and saddles.

Merlin gave the word. The brothers spurred their horses out of the bushes and charged the dark group, one on the right hand and one on the left. In the darkness and confusion the enemy knights fought each other and no man knew who was his foe. Balin and Balan dealt such terrific strokes that when the escort finally broke and fled

They handed the wounded rebel over to the astonished porters

galloping down the track there were forty dead and dying on the ground.

They found Rience where he had fallen, badly wounded. He yielded himself their prisoner, and they made a rough litter for him drawn by horses, and set out at once to retrace Balin's journey back to King Arthur's court. In the early dawn they reached the palace. Balin would not go in, since he had been dismissed in disgrace, but they handed the wounded rebel over to the astonished porters at the gates and told them to take him to the King. Then they withdrew and found lodgings in Camelot.

King Arthur received Rience. 'Sir, you are welcome; what chance brought you here?' he said.

'Sir,' said Rience, 'an evil chance.'

'Who won you?'

'Sir, the knight with the two swords and his brother, who are two marvellous fighting knights.'

'I do not know them,' said Arthur, 'but I am much indebted to them.'

'Ah,' said Merlin, who stood suddenly beside them, 'I will tell you. It is Balin, who achieved the sword, and his brother Balan, a good knight; there lives no better for skill and worth, but, alas, he will not live long.'

'Alas,' said King Arthur, remembering the great figure of the prisoner from the north, 'that is a pity. I am much indebted to him, and I have not deserved such goodness from him.'

CHAPTER 5

SIR BALIN AND THE DOLOROUS BLOW

SIR BALIN had not understood Merlin's prophecy about the dolorous, or grievous, blow he would strike with the sword he had won. He did not even believe Merlin, but the wizard had spoken truth. There were strange things in the Britain of King Arthur's day, things of which Balin knew though he paid little attention to them. These things are what are called the Hallows.

The chief of them was the cup out of which Our Lord drank at the Last Supper with His disciples and in which blood was caught from His wounds on the Cross. The second was the lance with which His side was pierced. The cup was called the Holy Grail, and was said to have been brought to Britain by Joseph of Arimathea after the Crucifixion. Joseph had been to Britain before. It is said that he was the uncle of Mary, the mother of Jesus, and that he made his living in the tin trade. The chief tin mines of the world were in Britain, and so Joseph came here regularly. The people who live round the tin mines of Cornwall and along the coast of Somerset keep the tradition that Joseph brought with him his niece and her son Jesus, and that they all wintered somewhere in those parts. It is said that Jesus came back to Glastonbury when He was a grown man, before He began His teaching life of which we read in the Gospels, and lived there for a time.

Perhaps it was because of that connection that Joseph came back to Britain after the Crucifixion. He had to escape from Jerusalem because he was a friend of Jesus, and he took with him the holy cup and the lance and part of the crown of thorns. In those days the sea covered a great part of the land as we know it now, and Joseph's ship sailed through the tidal marshes right up to Glastonbury. There he landed and made himself a home. He built a little church to house the Holy Grail, and he planted the spray of thorn. It grew, and has had cuttings taken of it through all the centuries, and to this day flowers in Glastonbury not in the spring but at Christmas.

Britain was now chosen out as a holy land. Strange things happened, and heavenly things and beings began sometimes to be seen. The fame of these things spread over Europe, and people came from many countries to live in this holy land and to see the Holy Grail. But after Joseph's death people tried to steal the cup, because they thought they could make it work magic for them, and so true lovers of the Grail hid it and kept it secret. Every one knew of it but none was sure where it was. Sometimes it would appear on the altar during the service of the Eucharist, and show itself to every one, and then disappear. Sometimes it appeared in a castle hall after dinner, or to any good man while he prayed. Sometimes the lance was seen with it, its point always flaming where it had pierced the side of Our Lord. Sometimes angels or heavenly beings, men or young girls, were seen with the Hallows, and many other signs and wonders, which we shall read of later. But in whatever form they appeared, they always meant that men were in the presence of heavenly things, and sometimes of Our Lord Himself.

During the years of war and trouble before King Arthur won back the holy land of Britain for Christ, the Hallows had not been often seen. But as the worship of Christ was restored they began to appear again. They chose the castle of Carbonek for their chief haunt, and its lord Pelles became known as the Keeper of the Hallows. The nearness of these holy things gave men unusual powers but did not make all men good. Pelles was good, but he had a brother Garlon who was able to make himself invisible and used this power to win battles and kill men unfairly. He made himself the terror of the countryside, until one day he met Sir Balin.

After Sir Balin and his brother Sir Balan had captured the rebel Rience for King Arthur, Sir Balin had been forgiven the killing of the Lady of the Lake and taken back into the King's service. One day he was bringing a knight under safe conduct to the King, and as they rode near the town of Carbonek the knight reeled and fell from his horse. No arrow had flown and Sir Balin had seen no enemy, but there was a sound of hoofs, and in the breast of the dying man there stuck a spear.

Sir Balin pulled out the spear, and swore to avenge the death of the knight under his protection. As he rode on to report this strange event to the King he met a knight who joined him in his quest for the unknown killer. As they went by a hermitage outside a churchyard, another spear driven by an invisible hand struck down the second knight. The hermit and Sir Balin buried the knight, and the hermit told him that the murderer was called Garlon, and that he was not always invisible except for his face, which was always so dark that it could not be recognized. Sir Balin swore to hunt him down and kill him.

He arrived at the castle of Carbonek, famous for the Hallows. But Balin's mind was not on them but on killing his enemy. He was well received and taken in to supper. Balin refused to part with his sword but went in armed to the hall. As he sat eating he searched the rows of faces intently.

'Is there a knight in this court whose name is Garlon?' he asked his neighbour.

'There he goes,' was the answer, 'him with the dark face.'

Balin drew a deep breath. 'Ah,' he said quietly, 'is that he?'

Garlon saw that he was watching him, and came over and struck Balin on the face with the back of his hand and said: 'What are you staring at me for? Eat your food and mind your own business.'

'You speak good sense,' said Balin. 'I will mind my business that I came here for,' and he rose up and cleft Garlon's head to the shoulders. Then he snatched the truncheon of the spear which had killed the first knight and thrust it into Garlon's body.

At this killing of the lord of the castle's brother the hall was in an uproar. Every one set on Balin, whose huge figure towered over them all. Pelles came striding down and thrust them all aside and said he would kill his brother's slayer himself. He seized a weapon and at the first blow splintered Balin's sword. But Balin broke away and ran from the hall in search of arms, racing from room to room and finding none. Pelles pursued him hotly. Up the winding stairs leaped Balin, and as he ran the sounds from the hall died away and there was a deadly quiet, with only the sound of Pelles's feet behind him. Balin remembered the Hallows, but he was more afraid of Pelles. If only he had a sword in his hand, or even a spear! He flung open a door, and stood amazed. The room was hung with silks such as he had never seen; there was a bed covered with cloth of gold, and a figure stretched silently on it; and a table of pure gold standing on four legs of silver, and upon the table a marvellous spear strangely worked. Balin knew that he was in the presence of the Hallows, but the sight of the spear took all thought from him. He seized it, and turned on Pelles and ran him through the thigh. There was a terrific thunderclap; Pelles fell to the ground. Crash followed crash, and the walls and roof of the castle came toppling down. The ceiling of the room fell in and buried both Balin and Pelles in the ruins.

After three days came Merlin, who rescued Balin from the room. He told him that this was the dolorous blow which had been foretold for him, for the spear was the spear with which Our Lord had been pierced on the Cross, and Balin had used a heavenly thing for his own earthly need. It was Joseph of Arimathea who lay on the bed of gold. Pelles was of Joseph's family, and so had become Keeper of the Hallows. The presence of the holy things had preserved all these years the body of Joseph who had first been their guardian. Until now the Hallows had kept themselves apart from the sinful world, showing themselves to men of true hearts who loved God and tried to follow Him. But Balin had involved the holy spear in an earthly quarrel, and so had brought the Hallows into the sinful life of the world. The first results had been the wounding of Pelles, the good knight, the destruction of the castle, and a coming of sudden death and disaster over the whole countryside. Only those who truly love God can live well with heavenly things; sinful men destroy themselves by them, as Balin destroyed himself by using the spear to save himself.

He was not destroyed immediately. Merlin told him to come away, for no one could yet heal Pelles's wound. He said that the Hallows now loosed upon the world would move among men for their appointed time, and men would be tormented by this glimpse of heavenly things which they could not live with happily because of their sins, nor ignore because of the longing of part of their nature for good. But after years of trouble and sorrow there would come the High Prince Galahad, the knight who would be truly single in heart towards God, and to whom the heavenly things would be natural and happy. He would heal Pelles's wound, and bring the history of the Grail to an end, and heal the land of the effects of Balin's dolorous blow. But until this long history had been lived through there was nothing to be done for Pelles.

Merlin led Balin out through the ruins and showed him the hall where the fallen roof had killed every one.

Balin got on his horse, and said to Merlin: 'In this world we shall never meet again.' He rode away, knowing that his end was near. One day he heard a horn blow the *morte*, or notes for the death of the quarry in hunting, but there were no riders and no hunt in the woods.

'That blast,' said Balin, 'is blown for me, for I am the prize and yet I am not yet dead.' He came to a castle where he was made welcome, but was told that if he wished to go on he must fight with a knight who lived on an island near by and would let no one go by without a challenge.

'That is an unfortunate custom,' said Balin, 'for travelling men are often weary and their horses too; but though my horse is weary, my heart is not. I would be glad to find my death there '

'Sir,' said a knight, 'your shield is not good, I will lend you a bigger; please take it.'

Balin took the shield, which did not carry his own device, and went out. When he came to the island he embarked his horse and himself in a boat and went over the water, and on the other side he met a damsel who exclaimed with pity and grief that he had left his own shield behind. Balin saw that he could do nothing right, but his courage did not fail. He knew that he was near death. In his mind rose up the mountains of his home in far-off Northumberland.

'I am sorry that I ever came into this country,' he said, 'but I may not turn back now for shame, and whatever will happen to me, be it life or death, I will take the adventure that shall come to me.' But he did not know what final grief lay before him. He looked over his armour, blessed himself, and mounted on his horse.

Out of the castle came riding a knight all in red, on a horse with red trappings. It was Balan, searching for his brother. He too had been tricked by the people of the castle, who hated all good knights, and had been persuaded to carry a shield not bearing his own device. He looked eagerly at the advancing knight, but as he saw the shield he knew it was a stranger's. So they charged upon each other, the two best fighters of the day. At the first shock they unhorsed each other. Balin, weary with long riding, was badly bruised, and Balan was first on his feet. They drew swords and set to. They smote each other tremendous blows, trampling to and fro until the ground was all mud and blood. Each gave the other seven great wounds, of which one would have killed any ordinary man. Never had either of them met such an enemy.

At last the mighty Balin began to wear down Balan, until the red knight withdrew for a breathing space, and lay down. Balin lowered his sword and went over to him.

'What is your name?' he asked hoarsely, 'for till now I never found any knight who matched me.'

'My name is Balan, brother to the good knight Balin.'

The world went black before Balin's eyes. 'That I should ever see this day!' he said, and fainted on the ground. Balan crawled on all fours to him, and took off his helmet, but did not recognize him, so cut and bloody was his face.

Balin recovered consciousness, and said: 'O Balan, my brother, you have slain me and I you, wherefore all the wide world shall speak of us both.'

Thus they died, Balan first, and Balin at the following midnight.

In the morning came Merlin, who wrote on their tomb their names, and that Balin the Savage was he that struck the dolorous blow. He took the fatal sword which Balin had taken from the damsel and refused to restore to her, and he told the people of the castle that no one would be able to handle it but the best knight of the world, either Sir Lancelot or Sir Galahad, his son. Merlin left the scabbard in the island, and he made a bridge of iron and steel over to the island of only six inches breadth, over which no man could pass unless he was a knight without villainy or treachery. So the scabbard was left to await such a finder. The sword itself Merlin caused to be put in a red marble block standing upright as huge as a mill-stone, floating on the water. Merlin set the enchanted sword on its journey along the waters of Britain until the right man should handle it.

CHAPTER 6

THE MARRIAGE OF ARTHUR AND THE FOUNDING OF THE ROUND TABLE

FOR some years after he became king the fight to drive out the heathen and restore order in Britain took up all King Arthur's attention. But gradually he gathered good knights round him and set up a court and a government, and enforced his rule through the whole kingdom. At last there was happiness and order in cottage and castle. The fair-haired lad who had been acclaimed king that summer day in the London churchyard had grown into a bearded man, tall and handsome, stern to wrongdoers, quick and gentle to the good and to all weaker than himself or those in any kind of need.

Now his knights begged him to marry and make his court one which should spread gentle manners and courtesy through all classes. On one of his adventures Arthur had met the Lady Guenevere, daughter of King Leodegrance of the land of Cameliard. He had never forgotten her, though he had hidden his thoughts in silence. Now he asked Merlin to go with a train of knights to the court of King Leodegrance to ask for the hand of Guenevere for King Arthur.

'This is the best news I have ever heard,' replied Leodegrance. 'I shall send him a present that will please him, for I shall give him the round table that Uther Pendragon gave me. When it is fully seated it holds one hundred and fifty knights. I have one hundred good knights, but I lack fifty, for so many have been killed in the wars.'

So they made ready for the return journey. When King Arthur heard that Guenevere was coming his heart was filled with joy. He chose his best friend and chief knight, Sir Lancelot du Lac, to ride to meet her and bring her on her way.

It was a fine summer morning when the two companies met. Guenevere rode on a white horse bridled with gold. She was dressed in green and gold and was more beautiful than any woman in the world, and under a blossoming apple-tree she met Sir Lancelot. He was in full armour, but with his vizor up so that she could see his dark face, already marked with scars of fights. From that moment they loved each other, and Guenevere knew that her new life would be among friends.

The journey to Camelot was all gaiety and festival. Every evening the tents were put up in a sheltered spot in wood or valley, and supper was spread in great magnificence on silver dishes on the ground. The knights and ladies reclined on cushions while musicians played sweet music under the boughs, and a ring of sentries kept guard. Stories were told, or one of the ladies would take a harp and sing. Slowly the light faded and the stars came out and every one retired to their tents to sleep. In the morning there was a bustle of horses and men, of the striking of tents and wagons being packed, and off the whole company would go, chattering and laughing in a manner unlike the usual armed and alert expeditions of the knights. Sometimes the best route was by water, when the King sent barges to meet them, and they embarked and went gliding along the river, with the notes of the harpers sounding across the water and carried from one barge to another.

They arrived at Camelot (which some call Winchester), and there Arthur and Guenevere met again, under a canopy whose floor was strewn with flowers. The knights saw that the new Queen was 'fair of face and courteous, very gracious of manner, and came of a noble house. Marvellously dainty was the maiden in person and vesture; right queenly of bearing; very sweet and ready of tongue.'

The marriage and coronation followed as soon as possible. The Round Table was set up in the great hall and seats made for it. King Arthur had a plan for this table. He meant to have the knights who sat at it sworn to the highest standard of thought and living, a life in Christ in thought and action. It was to represent a perfect world, where love and goodness should move in a power which should spread out through every vein of life in Britain. As his marriage was to be this in the King's own life, so the knights of the Round Table were to be that power throughout his kingdom.

When the table was ready the Archbishop of Canterbury blessed the seats with great ceremony, and set the knights each man in his seat, or siege. While this was being done thunder was heard in the hall, and rolling music. Some men said the roof seemed to dissolve into cloud and become part of the heavens, and music came from thence. Every man's heart was filled with ease and joy, and the King's face was lit by a heavenly light.

When the strange sounds ceased, Merlin, standing by the King's chair, said to the new knights: 'Fair sirs, you must all arise and come to King Arthur to do him homage.' So they rose, and while they were kneeling before the King Merlin saw each man's name appear in letters of gold upon his siege. Three were left empty, and over one was written: 'The Siege Perilous.'

'What does this mean?' asked the King.

'Sir,' said Merlin, 'no man shall sit in those places but the two of best fame in any year. But in the Perilous

Siege no man shall sit but one, and if any one is so bold as to try to sit there he shall be destroyed, and he that shall sit there shall have no equal.'

The King saw that the table was no longer an ordinary table, planned by himself, but one with which God had chosen to be concerned. He felt that it was another blessing on his kingdom, as well as the Hallows.

Next day was the wedding-day, and at a great meeting in the morning the King arranged the ranks and grades of all his knights. His nephew Gawaine was there, son of his sister Queen Morgause of Orkney. Her husband King Lot had been killed by Pellinore, and she ruled in far-off Orkney with her sons Gawaine, Gaheris, Agravaine, Mordred, and Gareth. Gawaine and Gaheris were attending on King Arthur as his subjects, Gawaine a princely and ambitious knight, Gaheris as yet only a squire.

Pellinore was also at the wedding. He was a friend of Arthur's now that he had given up his fierce ways and used his strength to protect the countryside instead of attacking it. Merlin led him to the siege next to the two empty ones and the Siege Perilous, and said: 'That is your place, and you are most fit to sit here of any that are present.'

At this Gawaine's face darkened. Later he made his way through the knights to the group of squires and drew Gaheris aside.

'That knight is given great honour,' he whispered, 'which makes me very angry, as he killed our father. So I shall kill him.'

'Do not do it now,' said Gaheris, 'for I am only a squire, but when I am a knight I shall want to have my revenge on him too.'

'Very well,' said Gawaine.

The King was unaware that the first split had begun at the very setting up of the table. He had forgotten Merlin's prophecy about the son of his sister who would destroy the kingdom, and Merlin did not tell him twice.

But outwardly all went well. In great splendour the King was married to the Lady Guenevere in the cathedral of St. Stephen in Camelot. Then the King established all his knights. He gave lands to the poor ones, and made them an equal fellowship, none above or below his brother, as by the roundness of the table there could be no first seat or last. He gave them a rule of life: to follow Christ, to do no murder or evil deed, and to be true to the King; never to be cruel, but to give mercy to any who asked, on pain of losing their place in the brotherhood of knights; always to help women of all ranks in any kind of need; and not to take part in an unjust cause for any threat or bribe. All the knights of the Round Table swore to keep this rule, and every year they renewed their oath at the feast of Pentecost.

CHAPTER 7

THE CORONATION OF ARTHUR

THE chronicle of Wace tells us that the young Arthur 'was a very virtuous knight, right worthy of praise, whose fame was much in the mouths of men. To the haughty he was proud; but tender and pitiful to the simple. He was a stout knight and a bold; a passing crafty captain, as indeed was but just, for skill and courage were his servants at need; and large of his giving. He ordained the courtesies of courts, and observed high state in a very splendid fashion.'

He had had a crown placed on his head when he was first acknowledged to be king at fifteen years old, but since then he had fought great wars and won back many lands to obedience to the Crown. Now the time had come for a public coronation, at which all the princes and chiefs who held their power from the King should come and give honour to him. The young Queen was to be crowned too, and the occasion was to be one of the utmost magnificence and rejoicing.

The place chosen was Caerleon on Usk, in the stronghold of Wales into which the heathen Saxon never penetrated. The name meant 'castle of the legions,' for Caerleon had been a city since the Roman days. Now it was richer than all the cities of Britain, which had been looted and burned in the ceaseless wars. Pilgrims said that the mansions of Caerleon were better than the palaces of Rome. The River Usk flowed broad and clear on one side. Fertile fields spread round the river, and the storehouses and barns of the city were large and full. There were two big churches, one named St. Julius the Martyr and one St. Aaron. Round the worship in these churches many learned and holy men had gathered, so that the fame of Caerleon as a centre of worship and learning and music had spread overseas. The Archbishop of Caerleon, Dubricius, was a wise and good man who by love and prayer healed the sick and gave good counsel to the King.

It was indeed a place worthy for a gathering of princes and the coronation of the King. The date was fixed for Pentecost, or Whitsun, in the fine summer weather, and every lord and chieftain in Britain was bidden to be in Caerleon that day to see the King crowned and to acknowledge their obedience. Not only the earls who ruled over counties, but the captains and knights of the King's armies came, before whom the Saxons had fled in battles all over Britain.

The lords of the outer isles off the coast came too, either as subjects or guests of the King, chieftains from Galway and the Hebrides, Frisian and Danish jarls, and the horned helmets following Malinius the stranger King of Iceland. Acil the Dane and Gonfal came, suspicious of every man, yet amazed in reluctant wonder at the magnificence of Britain.

Princes from the continent of Europe came too: Ligier, Duke of Burgundy, Holden, Earl of Flanders, Guerin, Earl of Chartres who brought with him the twelve peers of France, Bedevere, Duke of Normandy, Hoel of Brittany, and many others. Even the dark haughty faces of lords from far-off Spain were seen among the throng. Never was seen such splendour of armour, horses, and clothes. Even the harness of the horses was jewelled and finished with gold, and every lord wore silk and linen, velvet and fur.

The city was full to the last attic. Servants of the court were busy from morning till night making ready for the guests and seeing that each was housed according to his rank. Each lord brought a train of followers, and all were on horseback. Soldiers went to and fro finding lodgings. In every street and courtyard were squires leading war-horses, pack-horses, and ladies' palfreys, saddling and unsaddling them, polishing the harness and gold trappings. There was a smith and forge on every corner.

Inside the houses the same bustle went on. Houses were cleaned from top to bottom, spread with fresh reeds, hung with arras taken from stores in deep chests. Pages, chamberlains, and maids scurried about from morning till night, fetching water, linen, baggage, brushing and folding cloaks and tunics and hose, carrying loads of fur and armour, stitching and mending, running on errands.

When the morning of the coronation came, a procession of archbishops, bishops, and abbots went to the palace to fetch the King. Then the pageant proceeded through the streets from the palace to the church of St. Aaron. In front came the four chief men of Britain under the King, carrying swords to show the power of the Crown, the Prince of Scotland, the Princes of North Wales and of South Wales, and Cador, Duke of Cornwall. Then came the King, between the two archbishops; then the bishops and abbots and the long train of lords and princes.

While the King's procession was making its way through the cheering crowds another was setting out with the Queen Guenevere. In front of the Queen walked four ladies, the wives of the princes who went before the King. They carried white doves in their hands to show the mercy of the Crown. Behind her came the whole gay company of damsels and ladies, the noblest fellowship of women in the whole kingdom. All eyes followed the Queen's procession as it wound its way towards the church, hastening a little in case it should miss the opening of the service.

Now in both churches the ceremony began, with all the devotion and splendour that prayer and music could give. Never were there such singers as the Welsh, and as the organ and the voices of the choir rose in beautiful and cunning harmonies the experts from the courts and cathedrals of Spain and France listened enraptured. The knights went from one church to another, to delight their ears with the singing and their eyes with the loveliness of the ladies. The fame of the music and the singing at this coronation was carried across Europe.

When all was over and the last words chanted, the King and the Queen took off their crowns and robes of state and put on lighter ones for ordinary occasions. Then the two processions returned each to its own court for the banquet, for the Britons still kept the ancient custom, that when the feast was spread man ate with man alone and brought no lady with him to the hall. King Arthur altered this later, but not yet.

The King sat in his chair raised on a step above the rest of the room, at the head of the table, and all his knights and guests sat in order of their rank. The Round Table was in Camelot and not here in Caerleon. Sir Kay, foster brother of the King, and Steward of Britain, ordered the feast, clad in scarlet silk. An army of young pages in white ermine carried the dishes to and fro from the buttery. Sir Bedivere, the King's cup-bearer, ordered the serving of the wine, and another set of pages hurried at his direction to pour the red wine into golden beakers.

At the Queen's feast an equal magnificence was shown. The dishes and vessels were of the finest gold and silver. Every lady tried to be as courteous and noble as her lord was brave and honourable. The fame of Arthur's and Guenevere's banquets spread far and wide. The poorest peasant of Britain in his smock, it was said, was a more courteous and valiant gentleman than was a belted knight beyond the sea.

After the feasts were over the King and his fellowship went out into the fields for games and jousts. These went on for several days and all the people of the town took part. The lords and knights jousted together on horseback or on foot with the sword. Others shot with the bow, or threw stones from slings, or hurled darts. There were splendid prizes and the King himself gave each one to the winner and praised his skill. The ladies of the court climbed on the walls of the town and sat under canopies to watch the sports, and urged on their friends with clapping and cries. There were story-tellers, dice and card players, chess and draughts competitions; there were plays performed before the King; acrobats and dancing girls, weight-lifters, conjurers, trick riders, sellers of ornaments, toys, and charms. Every one could find something to enjoy, and wine from the King's butteries flowed freely in the tents.

The holiday went on for three days. On the Wednesday after Whitsunday, his coronation day, the King held a farewell meeting of all who had been asked to the ceremony. They had come from far, and now before they set out on their laborious journeys home the King thanked each of them, praised his courtesy in coming and the country he came from, and gave him gifts to carry back. The old chronicle tells us some of these gifts. 'To those stranger knights who for his love had crossed the sea on his behalf, the King gave armour and war-horse and golden ornaments, to their desire. He granted greyhound and hound, furred gown and raiment, beaker and goblet, lance and sword and quivers of sharp barbed arrows. He bestowed harness and buckler and weapons well fashioned by the smith. He gave bears and leopards, palfreys and pack-horses, chargers with saddles thereon. Yes, he bestowed on his servants the very richest and most precious of his treasure. Never a man of these outland knights, so long only as he was worthy of Arthur's bounty, but the King granted him such gifts as he might brag of in his own realm. And as with the foreign lords, so to the kings and princes, knights, and all his barons, Arthur gave largely many precious gifts.'

2

THE ROUND TABLE IN ACTION

CHAPTER 8

SIR LANCELOT

NOW the kingdom was won back from the heathen invader and the King was truly crowned. The wars were over, but a harder work now began, to govern the kingdom wisely and to build it up again in the service of Christ. The instruments of the King's work were his knights. On them depended his success or failure.

Chief of the knights was Sir Lancelot du Lac. He was the son of King Ban of Benwick, which some say was Bayonne in South-west France. He was called Du Lac, meaning 'of the Lake,' because it was said that when he was a baby he was stolen by the Lady of the Lake, and brought up in her country under the waters of a lake. He had great wealth and possessions throughout France, but although he was a king's son we do not know why he chose to serve King Arthur of Britain instead of the King of France. Indeed, his coming to court is only known by chance.

Some time later, when a young knight came for the first time to court wearing an ill-fitting coat, Sir Kay laughed at him. But Sir Lamorak and Sir Gaheris warned him against despising the young man. 'For, sir,' they said, 'if you remember, even such a one was Sir Lancelot du Lac when he first came to this court, and full few of us knew from whence he came; and now he is proved the man of most honour in the world.'

From this we know that he must have come unknown and in poor clothes, and won his fame by his own merits and not on the strength of his family or wealth. Later on his brother Sir Ector followed him—a different Sir Ector from the one who had brought up King Arthur.

Sir Lancelot went as a new knight with King Arthur on a two-year expedition into France, central Europe, Italy, and finally Rome, and returned from it the leading knight in the whole country, and the King's right-hand man.

He entered on the task of government, and was soon known as the chief man in the country after the King. No knight had ever defeated him in combat, and on horse or on foot Sir Lancelot was the champion knight of the world. He was the King's friend, and he had sworn a vow of service to the Queen. Although he would help any woman, he had sworn to be no other lady's knight but only the Queen's, and to serve her and the King all his life.

Soon after they all came home from the foreign war the King gave Sir Lancelot the task of looking after a certain part of the country and seeing that the laws were kept. He was to report on the state of the district and his doings there at the court at Pentecost.

The countryside showed the waste and damage that had been caused by the years of war before King Arthur had brought peace to Britain. No castle, farm, or house did Sir Lancelot find for many a mile where he might shelter at night. All was wildness and silence. At last he came on some cultivated land, and saw buildings. The house was built inside a protecting wall, with a gate leading in under a store-room. Here he was well received by an elderly couple and given food and drink for himself and his steed. When bedtime came his host led Sir Lancelot to the room over the gate. He unarmed and put his armour and sword beside him and was soon asleep on a cover thrown over a pile of clean straw.

Suddenly a violent knocking on the gate below awoke

Sir Lancelot du Lac

him. He ran to the window and saw by the light of the moon a knight, and three more riding down on him. The knight turned to face his pursuers and tackled them bravely. At this Sir Lancelot quickly put on his armour. He tied his bed-sheet to the window and threw it out and slid down it. Then he strode between the fighting knights. To his surprise he noticed the single knight's shield as that of Sir Kay, the King's steward. He leaped at the three knights, and in seven strokes had smitten them all to the ground.

'Sir Knight,' they said, 'we yield to you as to a champion of unmatched strength.'

He answered: 'I will not accept your yielding to me. You must yield to this knight, or else I will kill you.'

'Fair knight, we cannot do that, because we should have beaten that knight if you had not come.'

'Well, you can choose whether you will die or live. If you yield, it must be to Sir Kay.'

So the three yielded to Sir Kay, and Sir Lancelot ordered them to go to the court at Pentecost and yield themselves to the grace and mercy of the Queen, and say that Sir Kay sent them there as her prisoners.

Then Sir Lancelot knocked on the door with the pommel of his sword. Cautiously the old couple peeped out through the hatch. To their astonishment they saw the friendly face of their evening visitor, whom they had last seen going to bed in the gatehouse store-room.

'Sir,' said the old man, 'I thought you were in bed.'

'So I was,' answered Sir Lancelot, 'but I got out of the window to help an old friend of mine.'

Then he and Sir Kay were let in, and they all ate and drank again and went to bed in the best of spirits.

In the morning Sir Lancelot got up very early and left Sir Kay sleeping. He took Sir Kay's helmet and shield.

leaving his own in their place, said good-bye, and rode off.

When Sir Kay awoke and saw the famous shield with the leopards on it he laughed and said: 'Now he will upset some of the knights, because they will think he is I and they will be bold and tackle him. While wearing his helmet and shield I shall ride in peace; no one will dare to attack me.'

Sir Lancelot rode on for several days. He left behind the open country and entered a great forest. He met a lady weeping, who held his bridle and said:

'On your oath of knighthood, help my brother who is badly wounded and we cannot stop the bleeding. A sorceress living in the castle here told me his wound would never be healed unless I could find a knight who would go into the Perilous Chapel, and find there a sword and a blood-stained cloth which is laid over a wounded knight. A piece of that cloth, and the sword, would heal my brother if they touched his wounds.'

'This is a strange thing,' said Sir Lancelot. 'What is your brother's name?'

'Sir Meliot of Logres.'

'He is a knight of the Round Table, and I will do anything I can to help him,' answered Sir Lancelot.

He followed the lady's directions, and came through dismal woods to the Perilous Chapel. He dismounted and tied his horse to the gate. As he went into the churchyard he saw that the wall of the chapel was covered with shields nailed upside-down, showing that their owners had been killed. His eye picked out many that he had known well at court and in the wars. His face darkened, and suddenly he was aware that below the shields there stood a line of huge armed black figures, taller by three feet than any ordinary man, and he realized that these figures had accounted for the owners of all the shields. They made no movement, but a grin of triumph came over each face as they saw another victim approaching. Sir Lancelot felt a throb of terror, but he slung his shield before him and gripped his sword and strode on.

When he was only one step away from their swords, they suddenly broke before him and fell back. The chapel door was in front of him and he went in. The door shut behind him, with those huge figures outside, and darkness closed round him. But in a moment he made out a dim light, and going towards it he saw a figure lying under a silk cloth, with a sword beside it. Stooping down he cut off a piece of silk, and he felt the earth quake under him, and again his heart throbbed with fear.

Taking the sword he went down the chapel and opened the door. There were the grim figures, and as he stepped out they said: 'Sir Lancelot, put down that sword or you will die.'

'Whether I die or live you shall not get it from me by words or threats. Fight for it if you want it,' answered Sir Lancelot. He went straight through them and not one dared attack him.

Outside the churchyard gate a strange lady met him and she said: 'Sir Lancelot, leave that sword behind or you will die.'

'I shall not leave it for any number of threats,' he answered, whereupon she replied: 'If you had left it you would never see the court or Queen Guenevere again.' She asked him to kiss her, and he refused. She broke out in anger and amazed him by saying that all her trouble was for nothing, because she had made this chapel as a trap to catch him, and if he had given way to fear or weakness he would have fallen under her power and she would have killed him. But he had defeated all her spells.

'God preserve me from your cunning,' said Sir Lancelot, and he sprang on his horse and rode away. He found Sir Meliot's sister and they hurried to the castle where Sir Meliot lay, pale as death and almost dead from bleeding. One touch of the silk and the steel closed his wounds and restored him to health.

Great was the joy of the brother and sister, and they did all they could to thank Sir Lancelot. Not only had he saved Sir Meliot's life but he had broken the power of the sorceress whose spells had caught and killed many good knights. Sir Lancelot told Sir Meliot to come to the court at Pentecost and report to the King all that had happened. Then he continued on his way.

His next encounter was with another attempted trick, not of magic this time but plain murder. It was not for nothing that King Arthur had chosen his best knight to carry the King's law into this particular part of the country.

As he rode under a castle wall he heard a falcon's bells over his head, and an escaped falcon flew into an elm-tree trailing her long leashes. They caught in a bough and as she tried to flutter off she was jerked back and hung by the legs. Sir Lancelot was wondering how he could help her when a lady came hurrying out of the castle and called him by name.

'Sir Lancelot! Sir Lancelot! Help me to get my hawk back! If she is lost my husband will kill me, he is so hasty. As you are a true knight, help me.'

'What is your lord's name?' asked Sir Lancelot, still watching the hawk.

'Sir Phelot. He is a knight of the lord of North Galys.'

'Well, madam,' said Sir Lancelot, seeing that the hawk was in real danger of hurting herself, 'as you know my name and appeal to me as a knight to help you I will try and catch your hawk. But heaven knows, I am a bad climber and the tree is very high and with hardly any boughs to help me.'

A little reluctantly he dismounted and asked the lady to help him off with his armour. He put it in a pile with his arms, and clad only in a shirt and breeches began to climb the elm. He reached the falcon and managed to disentangle the leashes, which he tied round a stick, and then he dropped the stick with the struggling hawk attached to it to the ground.

As soon as the lady had picked up the falcon an armed man ran out from behind a bush with a drawn sword and shouted: 'Aha, Sir Lancelot, now I have got you!' and Sir Lancelot realized that the whole affair had been a trick, and he was caught in his shirt and without a sword. He was in much greater danger than he had been even from the knights in the enchanted Perilous Chapel. His eye rapidly reviewed the situation and the position of the branches below him and his pile of arms on the ground. 'Lady,' he called, 'why have you betrayed me?'

'She did as I told her,' said Sir Phelot, 'so there is nothing for it but your time is come and I shall kill you.'

'You would be shamed for ever—an armed knight to kill a defenceless man by trickery.'

'That cannot be helped,' answered Sir Phelot. 'Do what you can.'

'You will be for ever shamed for this. But at least hang my sword up on a branch so that I can get it and then kill me if you can.'

'Not I,' said Sir Phelot. 'I know you too well. You will get no weapon that I can keep you from.'

Sir Lancelot began to climb down. On his way he broke off a tough spiky branch. Sir Phelot watched him, gripping his sword. Sir Lancelot measured the distance from the tree to his horse with his eye, and climbed down.

Long before Sir Phelot expected it, he jumped from the tree, to the further side of his horse from the enemy. He had time to scramble to his feet before Sir Phelot had run round the horse, and Sir Lancelot leaped on him and smashed the sword out of his hand with his bough. He felled him to the ground and then seizing Sir Phelot's sword he cut off his head.

The lady screamed: 'You have killed my husband!'

'It is not I that am to blame,' answered Sir Lancelot sternly. 'You tried to kill me by lies and trickery, and now you have both paid for it.' He armed himself as fast as he could, fearing that Sir Phelot's soldiers might rush out of the castle on him. He got on his horse and rode away, thanking God that he had escaped that danger.

He continued his journeys through the countryside and after several other encounters he arrived back at court two days before Pentecost. 'The King and all the court were very glad,' says Malory. 'There was laughing and smiling among them, and every now and then came the knights who had been taken prisoner, and Sir Kay and Sir Meliot of Logres, and they all honoured Sir Lancelot. And so at that time Sir Lancelot had the greatest name of any knight in the world, and was the most honoured of high and low.'

CHAPTER 9

TALIESSIN

TALIESSIN was King Arthur's poet. As Lancelot expressed the King's will in action as his second-in-command, Taliessin expressed it in words. His poems told the deeds of the knights to the world, and the strange events which came upon the court, and tried to examine and explain them. From the beginning, power from God inspired the words of Taliessin.

In his own time he became himself a subject for poetry. The teller of his story in the *Mabinogion* says that Taliessin's mother Caridwen wished to be rid of him when he was born but could not bring herself to kill him because of his beauty. So she put him in a leather bag and threw him into the sea to the mercy of the Trinity on the 29th day of April.

Close to where she threw him in was the salmon weir belonging to a rich earl, Gwyddno. Every spring the great salmon came upstream from the sea, the noble silver fish making their way up to their native pools. Every May Eve Gwyddno gave the right to net and drag the weir to one of his friends, and usually a hundred pounds' worth of salmon was the result. This year Gwyddno gave the right to his son Elphin, who was the unluckiest man in Wales and for whom everything went wrong. His father wondered if this time his luck would turn.

When Elphin approached the weir on the soft spring evening of 30th April there was not a salmon to be seen. Only a leather bag floated against a weir pole. While his companions were whispering that Elphin brought bad luck wherever he went, he drew in the leather bag and opened it. When he and his friends saw the beauty of the baby boy inside they said: 'Behold a radiant brow!' and Elphin translated that into a Welsh word and said: 'Taliessin be he called.'

Elphin was good to Taliessin from the beginning. He carried him home very gently on his horse, and to his amazement on the way the infant uttered his first song. He assured Elphin that he would bring him luck:

'In the day of trouble I shall be
Of more service to thee than three hundred salmon,
Elphin of notable qualities.
Be not displeased at thy misfortune;
Although reclined thus weak in my bag,
There lies a virtue in my tongue.
While I continue thy protector
Thou hast not much to fear;
Remembering the names of the Trinity,
None shall be able to harm thee.'

When Elphin arrived home his father Gwyddno asked if he had had a good haul of fish. He said he had got something better than a fish, a poet, and he held up the baby.

'Alas, what good will he be to you?' exclaimed his father.

The baby Taliessin answered for himself: 'He will be more good to him than the weir is to you.'

'Are you able to speak, and you so little?' cried Gwyddno.

Elphin gave the baby to his wife, and together they brought him up with love and care until he was thirteen years old. All those years luck and prosperity were on Elphin's side. His animals were never sick, his land yielded big crops, he grew rich and respected. He believed

Taliessin was responsible, and even Gwyddno came to believe it. Every one was good to the boy.

When he was thirteen years old, and considered half grown up, they all went to spend Christmas with Gwyddno's brother Maelgwn, the chief man of the local countryside. All Maelgwn's relations and tenants and people came for the Christmas feast. There were twenty-four poets altogether, and they held a competition to judge who was the best. The best poems were to be one in praise of Maelgwn's wife and one in praise of his poets.

When they had finished their poems, before the prize was awarded, Elphin rose and said that his wife was as good as Maelgwn's and his poet a great deal better than Maelgwn's. His uncle was so angry that he instantly shut him up in a tower with heavy chains on his legs. No one expected to see him again. Then, after Christmas, Maelgwn carried out his tests of Elphin's challenge.

He sent his son Rhun to test the goodness of Elphin's wife. Taliessin took charge of the situation. He made his mistress change places with one of the housemaids, and when Rhun arrived the maid received him and he took her for the lady of the house.

At supper that night Rhun tried to make her drink too much, and succeeded. She fell asleep at the table, and as a proof of her drunken behaviour Rhun cut off her little finger on which was Elphin's ring.

Maelgwn was delighted. He had Elphin brought before him in chains, and the lord's wife and friends sat round ready to despise the man who had been so mistaken in his wife.

When Elphin heard the story and was handed the finger he kept his head. He examined the finger closely, and then said: 'I cannot deny my ring, for it is known by many, but I assert that the finger round which it is was never attached to my wife. Her fingers are so small that she could hardly keep this ring on her thumb, where she always wore it. This finger is the little finger of a hand, and the ring will scarcely pass over the joint. Secondly, my wife cuts her nails every Saturday, and you can see that the nail on this finger has not been cut for a month. Thirdly, this finger has traces of dough on it, and my wife has never kneaded dough since she was my wife.'

Maelgwn was very angry at Elphin's coolness, and swore he would not release him yet, but shut him up until he had made good his boast about the poet. So back went Elphin to prison, and he began to doubt his uncle's good faith, and to fear that he would never be released at all.

Meanwhile Taliessin left Elphin's house and came to the house of Maelgwn. He sat down in the dining-hall in a quiet corner near the place where the poets used to stand to sing and recite before the lord during the meal. When the heralds and poets filed in to proclaim the power and magnificence of Maelgwn, Taliessin pouted his lips and blew through his fingers at them. Nobody noticed him, and the procession marched up to the high table and lined up before the lord. But when the poets began to speak they could do nothing except pout and blow through their fingers. Maelgwn flew into a rage when this went on and on, and sent a squire to hit the leader on the head. At that the leader recovered the power of speech, and said their behaviour was due to a spirit in the hall, and he traced the spirit to the lad Taliessin.

So Taliessin was marched up in front of Maelgwn, who asked him what he was and whence he came. He answered as a poet, in verse:

'Primary chief bard am I to Elphin,
And my original country is the region of the summer stars;

. . . . .

At length every king will call me Taliessin.'

He went on in verse to speak of the origin of the poetic spirit, and Maelgwn and the assembled company heard the inspired song with amazement. But Maelgwn was angry because he was Elphin's poet, and he ordered his own poets to try to compete with him. But again they could do nothing but pout and blow. Maelgwn angrily asked Taliessin why he had come. The lad replied in verse that he had come to end the imprisonment of Elphin. Seeing that Maelgwn only set his face against him and was going to take no notice, Taliessin broke into a song of enchantment to raise a storm that would terrify him into submission. Wilder and wilder grew the song, faster and faster the words, as the sky darkened and a wind began to whistle through the hall, wrenching at hangings, slamming doors, bringing spears crashing off the walls. Above the noise of the storm shrieked the voice of Taliessin:

'One Being has prepared it,
Out of all creatures,
By a tremendous blast,
To wreak vengeance
On Maelgwn Gwynedd.'

Maelgwn sprang up trembling as the house rocked to the gale that tore through it at his name. He shouted to the terrified servants to fetch Elphin. As the storm died away, the chained prisoner stood before his foster-son. Taliessin sang a song of liberation which loosed the chains off Elphin's feet and made him a free man. Then he sang a song about poets, to prove that he was a better poet than any present. He sang it so well, and Maelgwn was so thankful that the storm was over, that they became friendly and made peace all round. Elphin's wife was fetched, and found to have no finger missing, and every one was happy.

Then Taliessin slung his harp on his back

After they had all gone home a race meeting was held and Elphin's horse stumbled. Taliessin told him to get his men to dig on that spot. They found a huge cauldron full of gold. Taliessin said: 'Elphin, here is payment for you for having taken me out of the weir, and for having brought me up from that time till now.'

Then Taliessin slung his harp on his back, said a loving farewell to Elphin and his wife, and set out to discover the world. He took ship from Wales, and by many adventures wandered south to Spain, and Rome, and Byzantium, studying in all places and events man and his burning heart. He became famous in many countries, but the fame of another man of Britain began to meet him on his travels, that of Arthur, the young king who had lately taken up the rule in his troubled land. He heard men say that Arthur had sworn to stamp out war and evil in Britain, and had founded a marvellous table of knights sworn to Christ, to strong and good living, to justice and mercy, and to the service of Christ in their fellow men.

One day there came a message from Arthur, King of Britain, to the poet of Britain, Taliessin. So he set sail, his harp on his back, and landed again in Britain and saluted his native earth. He took horse, and rode for the hills of Wales. As the blue-green hills and valleys closed about him, he knew that his wanderings were done. He rode fast to the King's camp at Caerleon on Usk. There he first saw the young King Arthur, tall and golden-haired, surrounded by knights of the Round Table, all young, all magnificent, all good. There was dark Lancelot fresh from France, red-haired Gawaine still speaking with the Norse accent of Orkney, Lamorak clear-eyed and warm with Welsh fire, and there at the King's hand was the flower of the west, young Guenevere the Queen.

Taliessin exchanged salutations with the company,

which, though young, was already famous, and they looked with wonder on the golden-tongued poet of the west. King Arthur asked him to take the Poet's Chair of the Round Table, and Taliessin accepted. He was led to the chair and seated in it, and from that day onward he remained the King's poet.

CHAPTER 10

SIR TRISTRAM

SIR TRISTRAM was called the second knight of the world after Sir Lancelot. He was born in Liones, or Lyonesse, which some men say was the land which once stretched between our Cornwall and French Brittany, and which on one Sunday morning was engulfed in a dreadful rising of the tide, and now lies under the sea. His mother was Elizabeth, the sister of King Mark of Cornwall, and his father Melodias, King of Liones under King Arthur.

Tristram's mother died when he was born, so he was called Tristram, which means 'a sorrowful birth.' Melodias grieved for his wife seven years, but then married again, and his new wife was jealous of Tristram because he would rule the land after his father and not one of her own sons. She put poison in the silver jug in the children's room, but her own son drank it and died instead. A second time she did it, but her husband was going to drink from the jug and she was forced to warn him and so he discovered her plot to kill Tristram.

She was sentenced to be burned, but when she was tied to the stake young Tristram knelt before his father and begged for her life. So she was spared, and loved the boy ever after, but Melodias thought it wiser to send him away for a while. He sent Tristram into France to learn languages and arts and deeds of arms. There Tristram learned the harp, and became chief among all musicians. He excelled every one also in hunting and hawking. He combined this with his music and invented all the hunting and hawking

See p. 79

They advanced and fought

calls on the horns and cries with the tongue which were used ever after by followers of the chase. He wrote the first book of the chase, describing every animal and how to hunt it, and put in order the whole business of the chase. The book of hunting and hawking was called the Book of Sir Tristram.

Finally, in deeds of arms he excelled all whom he met, for he was a lover of brave deeds as well as of sweet music and noble words. When he was nineteen years old he went back to Liones, and it was said that wherever he went he was loved by rich and poor.

At that time King Anguish of Ireland sent a strong knight named Marhaus to King Mark of Cornwall to collect tribute which Cornwall had paid to Ireland years before. Marhaus challenged any knight of Cornwall to fight with him to free Cornwall from having to pay the tax. No one dared to come forward, least of all King Mark. Tristram heard of this shame, and asked his father to let him go to the Cornish king and be knighted and take up the battle with Sir Marhaus. The more he was warned about the Irish knight's strength the more determined he was, and at last he had his way. 'And when King Mark and his barons of Cornwall beheld how young Sir Tristram departed with such a carriage to fight for Cornwall, there was neither man nor woman of honour but they wept to see and understand so young a knight to endanger himself for their right.'

The fight was long and fierce. Sir Marhaus wounded Tristram badly in the first charge, but the young man's strength carried him on. They fought for half a day, and then the older knight began to give ground. Sir Tristram smote him such a blow on the helmet that the sword went through into his skull and stuck so that he could not pull it out. As he wrenched, a piece of the steel broke off and stayed in Sir Marhaus's skull. The Irish knight turned and ran and Sir Tristram was left the victor. He had freed Cornwall from tribute for ever.

But he was very badly wounded, and the spear point had been poisoned. For a month he lay near death. Then he was told that he would never get well until he went into the country from which the poison had come. So King Mark gave him a ship and all the equipment he needed and he set sail for Ireland. As he sailed up a river he lay in bed and played his harp, and as the boat sailed past a castle by the riverside the King and Queen within the castle heard the merriest music that had ever been heard in Ireland until that time. They hastened to the waterside and found the wounded harper and brought him into the castle. He concealed his name because he had lately defeated the King's knight Marhaus, and Tristram now found not only that Marhaus had died of his wound, but also that he had been the Queen's brother, so that his life would have been short if the King had learned that it was he who had killed him.

The King had a daughter named Isoud, or Iseult, who was famous for her beauty and her skill as surgeon. Tristram was given into her charge to be healed of his wound. He repaid her by teaching her the harp, and they fell in love. At the court was a noble Saracen (or heathen knight) from Syria called Sir Palomides, who was also in love with Iseult and half willing to be baptized for her sake, in which case she would probably have had to marry him.

A tournament was arranged while Tristram was still sick, and on the first day Sir Palomides carried all before him. So on the second day, in spite of his wound, Tristram arose. In secret Iseult dressed him all in white armour, and he left the castle by a secret doorway and suddenly appeared to challenge Sir Palomides, 'and he came into the field as it had been a bright angel.' He charged the Saracen knight, who was victor of the field, and brought him out of the saddle to the ground. A roar went up from the crowd. Sir Palomides tried to withdraw from the field, but Sir Tristram forced him to stand and fight, and beat him to his knees. Sir Palomides was made to promise to leave Iseult alone, and to carry no arms nor armour for a year and a day.

After this Sir Tristram was well received by the King and Queen and lived in great happiness for some time hunting and hawking, and teaching the Irish the hunting craft he had invented. But one day while he was in his bath the Queen saw his sword, which was lying on his bed. A foot and a half from the point a piece was broken out of the edge. The Queen thought of the piece of steel which she had taken out of her brother's head before he died. She ran to her room and took the piece out of a box and fitted it into Sir Tristram's sword, and it was the missing piece. In her fury the Queen seized the sword and ran on Tristram in his bath. His squire flung himself on her and saved his life. Tristram then had to confess to the King that he was indeed the slayer of Marhaus. Although the King and Iseult loved him he had to leave Ireland. Before he went the Princess vowed to marry no one without his consent and they exchanged rings.

He went back to Cornwall and became the foremost man at court in fighting, hunting, and playing the harp. Now King Mark, his uncle, was seized with that black jealousy which poisoned his whole life. Where Tristram was, the King would never win, in jousting, hunting, or love. He became unable to rest until he had got rid of him.

Tristram had praised Iseult so highly that King Mark wanted to marry her. He thought if he sent Tristram back to Ireland he would be killed by some of Marhaus's relatives. So King Mark sent him to ask King Anguish for the hand of Iseult, and to bring her back to Cornwall to his court.

The young man set out. His ship was driven by a storm back to the English coast near Camelot. There he learned that King Anguish had arrived to answer a charge of treason before King Arthur, and could find no one to be his champion and fight for him. King Arthur's champion was Sir Blamore, cousin to Sir Lancelot and a renowned fighter. Tristram seized the chance to repay the Irish King for his hospitality in Ireland, and offered to fight for him. He defeated Sir Blamore, who refused to yield and demanded to be killed, but he would not kill him because he was of the family of Sir Lancelot, whom he admired more than any man in the world. 'For that gentle battle,' says Sir Thomas Malory, 'all the blood of Sir Lancelot loved Sir Tristram for ever.'

In great rejoicing the King and Sir Tristram sped to Ireland, where once again he found Iseult. When he asked her father for her hand for his uncle, the King said he wished it had been for himself. But he had given his word to King Mark and he would not break it. So Iseult made ready to sail with Sir Tristram to marry King Mark.

She took with her a noble lady named Bragwaine. The Queen secretly gave Bragwaine a love-potion which Iseult and Mark were to drink on their wedding-day. It would make them love each other for ever. On the journey, when Tristram and Iseult were down below in the cabin, they saw a gold flask containing what they thought was wine. It was the Queen's magic drink. Laughing, they said: 'Here is some special wine Bragwaine has been keeping for herself. Let us taste it.' So they drank it, and thought that no drink they had ever tasted was so sweet and good. The magic potion worked in them, and caused them to love each other for ever.

They arrived in Cornwall, and King Mark and Iseult were married. Soon afterwards Sir Tristram left Cornwall and went to Brittany. There he served Duke Hoel, who had been present at King Arthur's coronation, and became the leading knight in the land. But he was restless and returned to Logres. He landed in bad weather on an island off the coast of Wales. He met a knight, Sir Brandiles, who told him that the Round Table desired his fellowship, for he was considered second in knighthood only to Sir Lancelot. Sir Tristram served no one and held no vows of chivalry and it was felt that he should. But something held him back. King Arthur was in Wales at the time and was trapped in an ambush. Sir Tristram rescued him, but when the King asked his name he answered that he was a 'poor, adventurous knight' and would not take the chance to join the King.

But as time went by the fame of the King's court increased, and the deeds of the Round Table were on every man's lips. Not to serve the King became a sign of not being a true knight, while to be made a member of the Round Table became the ideal of knighthood. Sir Tristram decided to go to court, and to see if King Arthur would accept him.

The biggest tournament of the year was held by King Arthur at the Castle of Maidens. Every knight of fame was there wearing his colours and his arms. Sir Tristram came in disguise carrying a plain black shield and refusing to give his name. The first day of the tournament he overthrew every knight who opposed him. At the end of the day, when the prizes were awarded and he was victor, he rode away and hid in the forest while the King searched for him in vain. The next day he returned to the fighting.

He found Sir Palomides on King Arthur's side so he joined the other side. On the third day all the spectators were shouting for the knight with the black shield, and Sir Tristram surpassed all his former victories. King Arthur and Sir Palomides attacked him together. He dealt his old Saracen enemy three tremendous blows on the helm, shouting with each blow: 'Take that for Sir Tristram.' Then he forced his horse right up to Sir Palomides and seized him with both hands by the neck and dragged him from his horse on to his own saddle, and so rode with him for ten spears' lengths and flung him on the ground. The whole field roared with cheers.

Then Sir Lancelot cried: 'Knight with the black shield, make ready to joust with me,' and the highest test of fighting in all chivalry was on Sir Tristram. At the first charge Sir Lancelot's spear gave him a wound which nearly killed him. But Tristram kept his seat in the saddle and so the spear broke off. Seizing his sword with his remaining strength he smote Sir Lancelot three great blows on the helmet and could do no more. Blindly he rode off the field into the forest.

Sir Palomides rode after him. But, wounded as he was, Sir Tristram faced the Saracen and gave him another fall. Then he took shelter in a knight's house to recover from his wound.

The King and Sir Lancelot sent out search parties for the knight with the black shield. He was nowhere to be found. Sir Lancelot and nine others swore a vow to go on a quest for him and not to rest until they had found him and brought him before the King at Camelot.

When Sir Tristram was well again he set out in search of Sir Lancelot, who would bring him to the King. He did not know that Sir Lancelot was also looking for him. He went to the tournament at the Castle of the Hard Rock, hoping at last to meet him. Instead, he found an attack being made on Sir Palomides by nine knights, led by Sir Breuse Sance Pité. It was not a fair fight, and without hesitation Sir Tristram went to the help of the Saracen. No one could resist his blows and the nine knights fled. Then Sir Tristram would have fought Sir Palomides again but he saw he was too exhausted from the battle with the nine. So they made an agreement to meet in a fortnight by the tomb erected by Merlin over Sir Lanceor's body in the meadow by the river at Camelot, there to fight their quarrel out. Meanwhile Sir Tristram escorted Sir Palomides to safety out of reach of the nine traitor knights.

On the appointed day Sir Tristram rode into the meadow. He met a knight riding all in white armour and white colours, and took him to be Sir Palomides. They advanced and fought. After a few strokes Sir Tristram knew that a mightier man than Palomides was here, and he was forced to put out his utmost. Even so, for hours he could make no headway, though neither did he give ground. Then Tristram asked the strange knight his name.

'Sir Knight,' came the voice from within the steel helmet, 'my name is Sir Lancelot du Lac.'

'Alas,' said Sir Tristram, 'what have I done? For you are the man in the world that I love best!'

'Sir Knight,' said Sir Lancelot, 'tell me your name.'

'My name is Tristram of Liones.'

'Oh, heavens!' said Sir Lancelot, 'what a strange thing has happened!'

So the great knights met at last. They went to the tomb and sat down on it and took off their helmets to cool themselves, and told each other all the adventures which had led up to this meeting.

This was the end of Sir Lancelot's quest and of Sir Tristram's wanderings, for Sir Lancelot took him to

Camelot to King Arthur. The King came quickly and took him by the hand and said: 'Sir Tristram, you are as welcome as any knight that ever came to this court.' The Queen and all the ladies flocked to see the famous knight, hunter, musician, and lover of the Queen of Cornwall.

'Welcome,' said they all, and the roof rang with the answering shout of the knights.

'Welcome,' said King Arthur, 'as one of the best knights, and the gentlest of the world, and the man of most honour; for all manner of hunting you hold the prize, and of all measure of blowing the horn you are the author, of all makers of music you are the best; therefore, gentle knight, you are welcome to this court.'

So Sir Tristram was established as a knight of the Round Table, and his name was written over the seat which had been that of Sir Marhaus whom he slew.

He was there at the last meeting of the Round Table on that day of Pentecost when Sir Galahad was seated in the Perilous Siege and the Holy Grail shone in the air before all their eyes. But when the knights scattered on their search for the Holy Grail and the joy which they only knew when they beheld it, Sir Tristram was not among them. Perhaps the fatal love-potion had made him unable to forsake Iseult even for a quest of blessedness. Perhaps this hunter of the wild woodland, this harper from the rocks of Liones, was always a little outside the circle of knights with their vows of duty and service. No more is told of him, though a legend says that while he was seated playing on his harp to Queen Iseult, King Mark stole up and slew him by a traitor's stroke in the back.

CHAPTER II

SIR PALOMIDES

SIR PALOMIDES the Saracen had undertaken the quest of the Questing Beast. This beast was another marvel of Logres in King Arthur's day, and its meaning was never known. It had a snake's head, a leopard's body, a lion's hind quarters, and the feet of a deer; from inside its body came a hideous noise like that of thirty couples of hounds questing, and this noise the beast made wherever it went. So Sir Thomas Malory tells us, and the *High History of the Holy Grail* adds that the beast was as white as snow, of gentle appearance, with eyes green as emeralds, and that it fled perpetually from the hounds questing in full cry within its belly. It was a mysterious beast which puzzled all the knights, and Sir Palomides had sworn to undertake it as his quest and find out its secret.

He could not seek the Questing Beast all the time. In the intervals he pursued the art of jousting like all the leading knights.

One summer the King and Queen held a tournament in the fields outside Surluse. The Queen's knights issued a challenge, saying that the joust would last for eight days and they would 'joust against all men that would come.' Sir Palomides came, wearing on his shield the picture of the Questing Beast.

On the first day a damsel came to beg the Queen's help against Sir Goneries, who had taken all her lands from her. Sir Palomides asked leave to take up the challenge, and the Queen granted it. 'Each got a spear in their hands and met so fiercely that their spears were shivered. Then they seized swords and Sir Palomides smote Sir Goneries down to the earth. And then he raced off his helm and smote off his head. Then they went to supper.'

Sir Palomides fought so well that he became the chief figure in the lists. The Queen and Sir Lancelot sat on a raised platform to judge a contest between him and Sir Lamorak. In the middle Sir Lamorak hurled Sir Palomides and his horse to the ground, and Sir Lamorak's horse stumbled and fell on Sir Palomides. But even after this he fought so well that the contest lasted until the trumpets blew to lodging.

On the fifth day Sir Palomides had his greatest day. He knocked two knights from the King's side out of their saddles in quick succession; and when a knight went out to retaliate for the King's side he did the same to him. Sir Gawaine of the court side went out next, and Sir Palomides flung him and his horse to the ground. Mordred, Gaheris, and Agravaine met the same fate. The King's party began to get really angry. Sir Lamorak demanded if Sir Palomides would fight him again. 'Why should I not?' said Palomides. 'Then they hurled together, and broke their spears, and shivered them so that all the castle rang with their dints. Then each got a bigger spear, and they came fiercely together; but Sir Palomides's spear broke and Sir Lamorak's held. At that Sir Palomides lost his stirrups and lay right on his horse's back,' which counted as a win for Sir Lamorak.

Just then a message came from a maiden who was to be forced to marry a heathen knight, Sir Corsabrin, against her will. She could only be saved if some knight took up her cause and fought Sir Corsabrin. Sir Palomides at once took up the challenge. All the knights assembled to watch the contest. It was long and fierce. They fought on horseback and on foot. Sir Palomides demanded if his enemy would release the maiden. Sir Corsabrin was so enraged that he struck him on to his knees. But he leaped up and swung a mighty blow which laid Sir Corsabrin flat on the earth. Sir Palomides dragged off his enemy's helmet.

'Corsabrin,' he cried, 'yield, or you die now by my hand.'

'Do your worst,' replied Sir Corsabrin.

And Sir Palomides struck off his head.

From his dead body came such a foul smell as the unchristened soul departed that no one could go near it. That evening after the fighting the Queen spoke to Sir Palomides of it and urged him to be christened.

'I want you all to know,' said Palomides, 'that I came into this land to be christened, and christened I will be. But I have made a vow that I will not be christened until I have fought seven true battles for Jesus' sake.' Then he asked the Queen to dine with him, which she did, with Sir Lancelot and Sir Lamorak.

One of the most famous of his seven battles was the rescue of the Red City. Two evil brothers, Helius and Helake, had killed King Hermance and seized the Red City, his capital, which stood on the banks of the River Humber. Sir Palomides came to challenge them and to rescue the city. When the people saw him they were filled with joy, because he was a good knight, 'well made, clean and big, unmaimed in his limbs and neither too young nor too old. Though he was not christened yet he believed and was faithful and true of his promise.'

The brothers Helius and Helake boasted that they had slain King Hermance and said: 'Saracen Sir Palomides, we shall so handle you before you die that you will wish you had been christened.'

'It may well be,' replied the knight, 'for I would not die before I am christened. Yet I am not afraid of you two, and I trust to God that I shall die a better Christian man than either of you. And do not doubt,' he added, 'that either you or I will be left dead in this place.'

In the very first charge Sir Palomides ran Helake through the breast and killed him. But then began a desperate fight with Helius. Sir Palomides was flung off his horse and trampled on, and the fight went against him. Helius drove him about the field with terrible sword blows, so that all the oppressed people of the city wept to see their champion beaten. Sir Palomides was battered by a hundred blows and could hardly stand. But when he heard the common people weep for him he gathered his strength and looked Helius in the face and smote him such great blows on the head that he fell grovelling to the ground. Then he snatched off his helmet and cut off his head. So the tyrants were killed and the city set free.

Many other famous battles did Sir Palomides fight. His chief adversary was Sir Tristram of Liones, and the last of his seven great battles was fought against him. 'They came together as two wild boars, lashing together, wielding their blows as noble men that oft had been well proved in battle.' More than once Sir Tristram brought the Saracen to his knees. Yet Sir Palomides's sword thrust so shrewdly that Sir Tristram's shield was hacked away, and then the knight himself was wounded. In anger he rushed at Sir Palomides and flung him to the ground. He sprang up, but Sir Tristram's sword pierced his shoulder. A stroke from Sir Tristram twisted the sword from Sir Palomides's hand. If he stooped to pick it up he would be killed. Then Sir Palomides stood still and beheld his sword with a sorrowful heart. 'Now,' said Sir Tristram, 'I have you at a disadvantage. But it shall never be said in any court nor among good knights that Sir Tristram would slay any knight that is weaponless. Therefore take your sword and let us make an end of this battle.' But they both knew that they were such well-matched foes and such old acquaintances in arms that they had no more desire to fight. All quarrels were avenged in the blows and blood of the last battle.

Sir Palomides said: 'I require you, my lord, forgive me all that I have offended you; and bring me to-day to the nearest church and first let me be confessed and after see you that I am truly baptized. And then we will ride together to the court of Arthur, to be there for the high feast.'

'Now take your horse,' said Sir Tristram, giving him his hand, 'and as you say so shall it be,' and they forgave each other all their grievances. They rode to the nearest church, where the Bishop of Carlisle heard their story and baptized Sir Palomides. Sir Tristram, his old enemy and now fast friend, was his godfather.

They rode south to Camelot to be at court for the high feast of Pentecost. Great was the joy of King Arthur and all noble knights to hear that Sir Palomides was christened and the feud between him and Sir Tristram closed for ever. After the feast he returned to his quest, the Questing Beast, and we hear no more of him.

CHAPTER 12

SIR GARETH

GARETH, youngest son of the King of Orkney, was sixteen years old and ready to go to the court of his uncle, King Arthur. His half-brother Mordred and his three brothers, Gawaine, Agravaine, and Gaheris, had all gone years ago and had become well-known knights. Their father, King Lot, had been killed long before in battle and the Queen had been left alone to rule the stormy isles of Orkney. She was very unwilling to let her youngest son go, but he was determined not to grow into an uncouth islander, but to learn chivalry and to make his name in the world.

He did not, however, mean to arrive at court as the son of a king and brother of famous knights. He meant to keep himself unknown until he should have won his knighthood by his own merits. His brothers had been gone so long that they would not recognize him, and so he felt he could carry out his plan.

At the high feast of Pentecost, or Whitsun, in the fine summer weather, King Arthur held his court and Round Table at Kynke Kenadonne, a castle near the frontier of Wales.

Into the hall came two men, and on their shoulders leaned the best-looking young man that any one had seen, tall, fair, broad, and handsome. But he leaned on the shoulders of his friends as though he could not stand without them. He was about sixteen years old. King Arthur had been much the same age when he came to the throne, and fair and handsome like this young man. He had longed to do noble deeds, and he hoped now that this man had the same longing. Sir Gawaine and his brothers, red-haired and haughty, stared without recognizing the fair, gentle-looking stranger.

In accordance with the custom of the King on feast days, the stranger might ask a boon.

'Now ask,' said Arthur, 'and you shall have your asking.'

'Sir, this is my petition for this feast, that you will give me enough meat and drink for this twelvemonth, and then I will ask two other gifts.'

There was a stir of surprise and contempt.

'My fair son,' said the King gently, 'ask better; for this is only ignorant asking. My heart takes to you, and I am sure you come of a worthy family and will prove a man of great honour.'

Gareth longed to throw off his disguise and tell the King that he would be all he hoped of him, but he was a strong man, and having made up his mind to his plan he kept to it.

'Sir,' he said, 'let that be as it may. I have asked all I will ask.'

Arthur was puzzled, but he handed the young man over to Sir Kay, the steward, and told him to feed him and look after him as though he were a lord's son. Sir Kay and most of the knights were openly scornful.

'There is no need to go to so much expense for him,' said Sir Kay. 'I will bet he is lowly born and will never make a gentleman, for if he came of gentlemen he would have asked you for a horse and armour; but such as he is so he has asked. And since he has no name I shall call him Beaumains, or Fairhands, and I will have him in the kitchen and he shall eat fat meat every day, so that by the end of his twelve months he will be as fat as a pork hog.'

The less worthy knights sniggered, and the others said

nothing because they were sorry. Gareth's heart burned in him, but he kept his temper and made no reply. Sir Kay directed him to a seat at the hall door among the serving boys and lads, where he sat far from the King and knights and was soon forgotten.

So he lived in the kitchens and worked there, and slept at night as the kitchen boys slept. For a year he lived thus, and never once lost his temper or became out of humour. His size and strength made every one respect him, and though as a kitchen lad he was not allowed to take part in knightly exercises, he excelled in the other competitions such as wrestling or casting the heavy bar or stone. But every time that any knights were jousting and Beaumains was free, he was to be seen intently watching them and studying every stroke and rule of horseback fighting. He made friends with every one except Sir Kay, who went on sneering at him. When Beaumains won the competition in the whole neighbourhood for tossing the stone, Sir Kay only said: 'How do you like my kitchen boy?'

So the year passed until Pentecost came round again, and the King sat at the great feast. This time it was a damsel who came, and asked the King for urgent help. She said that her sister was being besieged in her castle by a knight called the Red Knight of the Red Lands, who was destroying her property and trying to force her to marry him. The King looked round his knights for one to go on this quest. But his eye was caught by the big figure of Beaumains pushing his way through the press from the far end of the hall among the kitchen boys. Beaumains came out in front of the King and stood by the damsel.

'Sir King,' he said, 'I thank you that I have been this twelvemonth in your kitchen and have had my full substance, and now I will ask my two gifts that are owing.'

The King told him to ask them. Beaumains first asked

See p. 101

Merlin led Vivien through the wood

that he might be sent on this damsel's adventure. She looked horrified, but the King granted it. Beaumains then asked that he might be made a knight by Sir Lancelot and by no one else. During his year in the service of the court, he had learned a great deal about every knight, and was convinced that none was the equal of Sir Lancelot.

The King granted him this also. The damsel was angry. 'Fie on you,' she said, 'shall I have none but one who is your kitchen page?' She went out of the hall in a temper and called for her horse to ride away. Then a message came that the horse and armour for Beaumains was ready for him, and every one was surprised to hear that he had any. But now was the moment to show the company the splendid equipment which the Queen of Orkney had given her son when he left home. The knights watched with amazement as the kitchen boy put on knightly dress and appeared before them like a prince.

So the new knight rode away after the damsel. Sir Kay rode after him and tried to stop him, but Gareth unhorsed and wounded him and rode on.

When he caught up with the lady she cried out: 'What are you doing here? You smell of the kitchen, your clothes are greasy with the fat from King Arthur's kitchen. Go back again, serving boy! You are only fit to baste joints and wash dishes!'

Not for nothing had Gareth learned to keep his temper. He answered: 'Damsel, say what you please, I will not go away for anything that you say, for I have undertaken to King Arthur to do this business for you, and I shall carry it through to the end or else die in doing it.'

At this she exclaimed in anger: 'Kitchen knave, do you think you can do my business? You would have to meet a knight that you would not dare to face for all the soup you ever drank.'

She spurred her horse, and Sir Gareth answered: 'I shall try,' and followed close behind.

Before long they met a man who was being attacked by six thieves. Sir Gareth rode hard at them. In three strokes he killed three, and the others fled. He chased them and they all turned and attacked him together but he killed them all. The knight who had been set upon brought him and the damsel back to his castle and put all he had before them. At supper he seated Sir Gareth next to the damsel. She said in disgust: 'Sir Knight, you are uncourteous to set a kitchen page next to me. He is more suited to killing a pig than to sitting with people of good birth.' The host was so ashamed by such rudeness to his rescuer and guest that he took Gareth away to another table and sat with him and left the damsel by herself.

The next day they rode away together, the damsel in front and Sir Gareth behind. They had many adventures, and in all of them Sir Gareth bore himself like a true knight, but the damsel still reviled him and called him 'kitchen boy' and still he gave her civil answers.

But gradually his good manners and brave fighting won her over, and she grew ashamed of her behaviour. They now approached the territory of the besieged lady, and the damsel made friends with Sir Gareth. She told him that her name was Linnet and her sister's Liones, and that the Red Knight who was besieging Liones was hoping to draw one of the famous knights of King Arthur's court to fight him, Sir Lancelot or Sir Tristram or Sir Lamorak. Sir Gareth sealed their friendship by telling her his real name and family, and proving to her that he was no kitchen boy.

Then they came out on to a plain, and saw the castle ringed round with tents and siege-engines and much smoke and noise. They passed a grove of trees, and from the trees were hanging by the neck forty dead knights in full armour, and their shields and swords hung from their necks and their gilt spurs were on their heels. Never had Sir Gareth seen such a shameful sight, for he had imagined that the Red Knight at least fought in knightly fashion and killed his enemies in combat. This was a shame he had not contemplated, and for a moment he was afraid. Linnet urged him to steel his heart and gather his courage.

On a sycamore-tree hung a tremendous horn, made of an elephant's tusk. Whoever wished to challenge the Red Knight had to blow the horn. Sir Gareth spurred his horse straight to the sycamore-tree and blew the horn so that all the siege and the castle rang with it. Knights started out of their tents, and the walls and windows of the castle were crowded with people.

'Sir,' said the damsel, 'here is your deadly enemy, and at that window is my sister, the Lady Liones.'

Eagerly Gareth followed her pointing finger. 'She is the fairest lady I ever saw,' he said. 'I ask no better quarrel now, for truly she shall be my lady and I will fight for her.' The Lady Liones waved to him and held out her hands imploringly. The Red Knight shouted to Sir Gareth that the lady was his and he meant to keep her, and that he had fought many fierce battles for her, as the forty knights hanging on the trees were witness.

Then they laid their spears in rest and charged. The force of their encounter hurled both knights from their horses, and they lay stunned on the ground. The onlookers thought that both their necks were broken. But they arose and took their swords and began a fierce contest. Blows rained on their helmets, pieces of their armour flew off, their shields and swords were hacked. They fought till past noon, and paused then for breath, standing panting, gasping, and bleeding, while the onlookers grew more and more excited. When Gareth took off his helmet to refresh himself he again saw the Lady Liones at the window, and she smiled on him so that his heart felt light and merry. Then he armed again and turned to the battle.

After a long time the Red Knight by a feint knocked Sir Gareth's sword out of his hand, and flung himself on him and they both fell sprawling on the ground. The damsel Linnet shrieked out: 'Oh, Sir Beaumains, where is your courage? My sister is watching, and she is sobbing and crying.' When Gareth heard this he made a mighty effort and leaped to his feet and seized his sword again. The fight was renewed, but this time Sir Gareth attacked with such fury that he smote the Red Knight to the ground and had him at his mercy.

He was very unwilling to spare the life of a man who had hanged forty knights, but at the request of all the watching knights and lords he did so on condition that the Red Knight and all his followers yielded to the Lady Liones and set her free. Then Sir Gareth took his horse and rode to the castle to meet the lady he had rescued after so many adventures. But he found the gate closed to him.

Liones, leaning from a window, called to him: 'As yet you shall not wholly have my love until you are among the number of the most honourable knights. Therefore go and strive in honour for a year and then you shall hear from me. Go on your way, and be happy, for all shall be for your honour and for the best, and a year will soon be done. Trust me, Sir Knight, I shall be true to you and never forsake you, but to my death I shall love but you and no other.'

So it happened, and at the end of a year the King himself attended their marriage in great splendour.

CHAPTER 13

GERAINT AND ENID

GERAINT, Prince of Devon, was one of the chief knights of the court of King Arthur. His lands covered the wide county of Devon, which was the frontier of Britain towards King Mark's kingdom of Cornwall and Lyonesse. He had been married a year to Enid, only child of Earl Yniol, whom he had met while on a mission for the Queen. He had been given lodging in the old castle and found that the family was too poor to have a servant in house or stable, and the daughter Enid waited on him and tended his horse. As she cooked and served supper in the one living-room of the ruined castle, Geraint fell in love with her. She wore a faded dress of which she was ashamed, but in which he thought her beauty showed more clearly than in the most splendid clothes. She too fell in love with him, and as the old Earl consented to the marriage, Geraint took her back to court with him in her old dress. The Queen immediately made friends with her, and gave her fine clothes and jewels, and the marriage was celebrated in splendour.

After six months at court Geraint took her back to his own land of Devon. But there, away from the manly rivalry of the court, he began to dote upon Enid so much that he neglected his duties and his ordinary life. He ceased to go hunting and hawking, or to practise in the tilt-yard and armoury, and became slack about sitting in the court of justice and seeing that right was maintained and wrong was punished throughout his county.

All this worried Enid. She could see that people were beginning to despise her husband, but she felt very shy about mentioning it to him. Geraint noticed her worrying, and jumped to the conclusion that she did not love him but was pining for some other knight at court. One day in mid June Enid woke early with the sweet summer morning, and lay awake reproaching herself for not having the courage to speak to Geraint about his indolent life. She felt she was not doing her duty, and Geraint awoke to hear her say to herself: 'I fear I am no true wife.' His false suspicions leaped on to the words. He was convinced that she loved someone else and his heart burned with jealous fury.

He got up, gave no explanation to Enid, but ordered his charger and her palfrey, told her to put on her shabbiest dress and follow him. He tramped through the sleeping castle to the stables. Enid, confused and frightened, put on the old dress in which she had first met Geraint. When they had ridden out of the castle and town into the dewy fields, he ordered her to ride well in front of him, and on her duty as a wife not to speak to him. So they rode all the morning. The day grew hotter, Enid grew tired, but Geraint did not relent.

In the afternoon the path turned into a cutting, and Enid saw four horsemen waiting behind a rock. They were obviously lying in ambush for a passer-by. She did not know what to do. Geraint had ordered her not to speak to him, but four against one when the one was not prepared was too dangerous. She risked his anger, and turned back and told him.

'You should have held your tongue as I told you,' he answered. 'I want silence, not warning. Even if you want to see me killed by these men, I do not care in the least.'

The horsemen, seeing that Geraint had been warned, dashed in on him. Fiercely he held them off, stabbing and hewing with his sword, and piercing one right through with his spear. When they were all dead, he took their arms and tied each set on to the saddle and gave Enid the reins of the four horses and told her to drive them all on in front. Her own palfrey, frightened by the fight, was hard to manage by itself, and four big horses as well was hard work. But the more helpless Enid looked the angrier she made Geraint, and he told her to hurry on ahead and keep silence.

So they set out again, Enid in a tangle with the horses, and rode out of the cutting across a plain, in the middle of which was a thick copse. Hiding in the edge of this Enid saw three armed horsemen, in ambush like the others. They watched with interest the approach of an unarmed woman driving four valuable horses with sets of arms. She remembered that Geraint had just fought four men, and was tired. She pulled her horses up and waited for him. He received this warning exactly as he received the other, and fought and killed the three men as if he did not care whether he won or not. To Enid's horror, he gave her the three new horses to drive as well, and told her to go on ahead and keep quiet.

The same thing happened again, but this time there were five horsemen. Again she warned him, and he answered: 'You continually do what I tell you not to do. I'll make you sorry for it yet.' He fell upon the five, overcame them, and added their horses to Enid's collection. She now had twelve to cope with, and it was the end of an exhausting day, and she and Geraint were tired out. They had nothing to eat, but they needed rest still more. They turned off the path, tied the horses, and slept exhausted in a little wood.

Next morning they set off again. They met a young lad carrying a blue jug with a bowl held on top of it, and a bag hung round his neck. Geraint asked him what he had there, and he said it was breakfast for the mowers who had been scything the hay since sunrise. He asked if Geraint and the lady would like some, and they thankfully got off their horses and ate and drank. Geraint asked the boy to find him lodgings in the nearby town, and gave him a horse and a set of arms for payment. After they were settled in their lodgings, they had to report to the chief man of the town, as the regular custom was. When the Earl saw Enid, and noticed that she and Geraint were on bad terms, he immediately began to want to get her away from him. As soon as the interview was over, Geraint and Enid pretended to go back to their lodgings for the night. Geraint then offered the landlord eleven horses and their arms, and the man guided them safely out of the town.

They made as good speed as they could through the dark, but as daylight came they heard horses behind them, and sure enough the Earl was in pursuit. Now Geraint had to fight with all the skill he had. It was a tough encounter, but finally the Earl was unhorsed and his undisciplined men had no spirit to go on attacking a knight of Geraint's standard, so they drew off. But Geraint was wounded, though he would not tell Enid. The wound bled and bled, until the sunny road began to swim before his eyes, everything went black, and he fell unconscious from his horse.

Enid did her best to get off his armour and find the wound and staunch it. Then as she could not lift him there was nothing to do but to sit down and wait for help. Plenty of people passed, but so lawless had Geraint allowed the country to become that a young woman weeping over a dead man by the roadside was nothing unusual, and no one stopped to help. At last came a troop of rough horsemen, with a wild-looking man at their head. It was a local chieftain, the Earl of Limours, coming out of his castle on a raid. His eye was caught by Enid, and he stopped to have a look at her. He was not interested in Geraint, but at her insistence he told two men to lay him in the hollow of his shield and take him back to the castle. He told Enid to go too and wait for him to come in from the raid.

All day she watched Geraint in the dirty empty hall of this robber stronghold. Starving dogs slunk round, and foul-looking women stared at her, but no one spoke or offered help. She dreaded the return of the wild Earl, yet she felt some good would come of it. At last in the evening there was a clatter, and the whole castle sprang to life to receive the returning raiders. People ran to and fro, cursing and shouting, carrying beer for the men to drink as they swung off their horses in the yard, and getting ready a large meal for them to eat.

No one took any notice of Geraint and Enid. Tables were put up and a rough, huge meal of whole joints of meat and quarts of beer and half-loaves of bread was put before each man. The dogs fought for bones, and the women, who were not fed till after the men, snatched the leavings off the plates. At last the men had eaten and drunk their fill. Then the Earl sent for Enid. He was annoyed to see her still in her old clothes and looking so sad. He told her to go with his women and get properly dressed for him to look at. She refused. He could not understand her. The women he knew only mourned a dead man until they had found a new live one.

He stared at her. She was much more beautiful than any one he knew, and in spite of her old clothes looked as if she had been brought up in quite different surroundings from those of the castle of Limours.

'Listen,' he said, 'I will treat you so that you need not be sorry whether that knight lives or dies. A good earldom and myself I will give you. Now be cheerful.'

The women behind his chair almost snarled at Enid as he said this. But she was only thinking of Geraint, and of her fear that he was dead.

'I swear I will never be happy as long as I live.'

'Well, eat something, anyway.'

'I will not,' she said, but he grabbed her arm and dragged her to the table and shook her as he held food against her face. The whole hall was watching now.

'I swear by heaven,' she gasped, 'that I will not eat until the man lying on that shield gets up and eats with me.'

'You can't keep that oath,' retorted the Earl. 'That man is dead already.'

'I will prove that I can,' she answered fiercely.

He seized a glass of wine. 'Drink this, and you will feel differently,' he said.

'I will not drink until he drinks with me,' she answered.

Furious, the Earl gave her a blow on the ear. For a moment she was stunned, and then she realized that he would never have dared to do it if Geraint had been alive, and she gave a scream.

That sound pierced through Geraint's faintness, and through the black wall of anger he had built up against his wife into the true love for her which still could save him. The drunken crowd saw what they believed to be a dead man leap up, sword in hand, run to the Earl and cut him right open with one terrific blow. With screams of terror the entire company fled, not so much for fear of a single living knight, as from what they took to be a ghost.

Geraint looked at Enid, and she saw all his love and repentance in his face. 'Do you know where our horses are?' he said.

'I know where yours is. I don't know where the other is,' she answered.

Hand in hand they went out to the stables, as dirty and badly kept as the castle, and took out Geraint's charger. Both of them got on to him, and rode out through an unguarded door.

They had time now for explanations and happy forgivenesses and renewals of love. They looked for a place where Geraint could have his wound attended to, and then by slow stages they rode home. Then Geraint mended his way of life:

> And there he kept the justice of the King
> So vigorously yet mildly, that all hearts
> Applauded, and the spiteful whisper died:
> And being ever foremost in the chase,
> And victor at the tilt and tournament,
> They called him the great Prince and man of men.
> But Enid, whom her ladies loved to call
> Enid the Fair, a grateful people named
> Enid the Good; and in their halls arose
> The cry of children, Enids and Geraints
> Of times to be; nor did he doubt her more,
> But rested in her fealty, till he crown'd
> A happy life with a fair death, and fell
> Against the heathen of the Northern Sea
> In battle, fighting for the blameless King.

CHAPTER 14

THE END OF MERLIN

MERLIN the wizard was a wise man nearly all his life, but when he was old he fell into foolishness. Perhaps he trusted too much in his own power, and so forgot the fear of God which is the root of wisdom. He fell in love with one of the beautiful young ladies of the court, called Vivien, a girl young enough to be his granddaughter. He became quite crazed about her, followed her about everywhere, and told her any secret of his magic she wanted to know. He knew he was making a fool of himself, and sometimes would summon his power against himself and get ready to destroy Vivien. One day she found him doing this, and made him swear a magician's oath which he could never break, that he would never use any enchantment against her.

Vivien had been brought up by the Lady of the Lake, Nimue, who was also a magician. One wielder of magic seldom likes another, and Vivien had grown up to have no love for Merlin. But as he was a famous figure at court, she was flattered and excited by his attention, and she also hoped to get some magical power for herself. It was not altogether comfortable to receive so much devotion from a wizard, and after a time Vivien became very tired of it. Then she grew frightened of him and said he was a devil's son, but neither neglect nor insult could move Merlin.

He was indeed impregnable from attack by other people. He knew this, but in his visions he could see that he was going to come to disaster. He warned the King, whose faithful ally he had been throughout his reign, and shook his head when he foretold how the King would need him when he was gone.

'Since you know what is going to happen, do something about it,' urged the King. 'Prevent the disaster by one of your spells.'

All traffickers in spirits know that they are controlled by the Ruler of Spirits, the Holy Ghost, but Merlin's pride in himself, which betrayed him into Vivien's hands, took from him that reliance on the Holy Spirit which could have cleared his vision. When the King urged him his eye clouded, his bearded face dropped on his chest, and his voice dwindled away to muttering. He became very angry, and took himself off in a cloud and reappeared suddenly beside Vivien as she was going for a walk, much to her annoyance.

However, her moment came. She had been storing up magic words and spells of a simple kind which Merlin had taught her, words which had power over elementary things like rock or earth. One day she was roaming in the forest of Broceliande with Merlin and he told her that there was an underground cave near by, with a small entrance that no one would suspect under a mass of rock. He offered to show her the marvellous subterranean treasures hidden in the cave, and she pretended to be very eager. Merlin led her through the wood and on the way a cloud of foreboding came over his spirit.

> So dark a forethought roll'd about his brain,
> As on a dull day in an Ocean cave
> The blind wave feeling round his long sea-hall
> In silence.

He was warned, but his reliance on himself was too complete. He went on, and led Vivien to the entrance in the rock. The moment he had stepped inside the mouth of the cave, she pronounced the magic word which had power over rock, and the two sides of the opening sealed together behind Merlin.

Only the person who had said the word could say the other word which would undo it. All his magic availed Merlin nothing in his imprisonment underground. Vivien ran from the rock in panic, and as she ran the thickets closed behind her and the place was lost for ever. Merlin is sealed up in the earth by his own folly and pride till all spirits meet before their Ruler. In the shakings of the earthquakes, in the groanings of the earth in lonely places, in the blasts of fire and water that start unexplained from the earth, the master of magicians groans and strives to ease his frantic heart.

3
THE QUEST OF THE GRAIL

CHAPTER 15

THE BIRTH OF GALAHAD

THERE came a hermit into the great hall at Camelot one Whitsunday when King Arthur was holding high court for the feast. The King loved to talk with wise men and hear them discourse, so while the meal was served the hermit stood by him and uttered visions and prophecies. He pointed to the Siege Perilous and asked if the King knew who would sit there.

'No,' said the King, looking round on his knights, who all shook their heads, 'we know not.'

'Then I know,' replied the hermit. 'He that shall sit there is yet unborn, and this same year he will be born, he who will sit in the Siege Perilous and win the Sangreal.'

The Sangreal was another name for the Holy Grail. Folding his arms and waiting for no dismissal the hermit then stalked out with slow and stately tread. It was a disappointment to every one that the adventure of the Siege Perilous was not going to happen for so long, as the person concerned was not even born. Sir Lancelot, who was used to being called the best knight in the world, was secretly relieved that the siege was not for him. He little thought how closely his fate was linked with it.

After the feast he rode out as usual on a quest to keep order in the countryside and enforce the law. Sir Lancelot was often involved in two kinds of adventure, one the ordinary kind belonging to every knight, such as fighting a law-breaker and enforcing justice, and the other such adventures as arose out of his own nature as the best knight in the world, who alone could undo enchantments and heal sicknesses of various kinds. On this occasion he met both types of adventure.

His quest took him to Carbonek, where he had not been for a long time. Scarcely had he ridden under the gate of the town when the people came crowding round his horse and led him into the main square in front of the tower shouting: 'Welcome, Sir Lancelot, the flower of knighthood! For by you we shall be helped out of danger!'

'What do you mean?' exclaimed Sir Lancelot.

They all went on shouting and at last one man stood forward and with his hand on the great charger's neck said: 'Ah, fair knight, within this tower there is an unhappy lady who has been there in pain many winters, for she is always boiling in scalding water. We know that it is you, Sir Lancelot, who will rescue her.'

'Well,' said he, 'tell me what I must do.'

So they took him into the tower and up the stone stairs to an iron door which they unbolted, and made him go inside into a room full of scalding steam. There he found a young woman sitting in a tub of boiling water, as naked as a needle. He took her by the hand and out she stepped. She told him that Queen Morgan Le Fay and the Queen of North Galys had put her in boiling water by a spell because she was called the most beautiful woman in the land. No one could undo the spell except the best knight in the world, and she had been there for five years. She was Elaine, daughter of Pelles, ruler of Carbonek and Keeper of the Hallows.

When she had dressed, Elaine went with her ladies and Sir Lancelot to the chapel to give thanks to God. She had already fallen in love with Sir Lancelot, and she remained in love with him all her life. She knew that she had not the least chance of marrying him because he was the true knight of the Queen, and though courteous to all women loved none but his lady. But although she had suffered so much under an enchantment in the last five years, she was not above trying enchantment herself on Sir Lancelot as she could not get him to marry her without it.

On coming out of the chapel Sir Lancelot was met by another deputation who said: 'Sir Knight, since you have delivered this lady, you must deliver us also from a serpent which is here in a tomb.'

'Sirs,' he answered, smiling, 'show me the tomb, and what I may do to the pleasure of God and of you I will do.'

On the stone side of the tomb was an inscription which said: 'Here shall come a leopard of king's blood and he will slay this serpent. And this leopard will father a lion in this foreign country which will surpass all other knights.' Sir Lancelot read this and said nothing. He was a king's son, son of King Ban of Benwick, and his shield carried leopards.

Sword in hand he raised the lid of the tomb. Every one screamed as out reared a dragon spitting fire out of its mouth. Sir Lancelot struck at it but its scaly skin repelled the blade, and its fire drove him back. Holding his shield with the leopards on it before him to keep off the fiery breath he sprang in and cut and sprang out of reach again, and so on for a long time. Elaine stood watching every stroke, noting the immense strength and the concentration of eye and hand and foot, and the fury with which he flung himself into the battle. No other fighter could compare with Sir Lancelot in action. Elaine determined on her enchantment. After a long struggle Sir Lancelot killed the serpent, and it occurred to him that the inscription on the tomb now definitely applied to him, though he did not understand it.

Pelles gave a feast to celebrate two such deeds of rescue in one day. The doors of the hall were thrown open and the people of the little town crowded in to stare at the famous knight, a visitor from the great world and the foremost knight in Christendom. Dressed in scarlet, with white ermine and gold upon it, the mighty figure of Sir Lancelot dominated the table. Yet he was as courteous to the least as to the highest, his eyes and face as attentive to the youngest as to Pelles or the Lady Elaine. He did not show off or boast, but treated every one as his brothers and equals, as he indeed regarded them as servants of Jesus Christ. During that dinner at least there was not a man who would not have died for him, nor a woman who was not in love with him.

This was Carbonek, the place of the Hallows. In such a power of love the Holy Grail was almost certain to delight to appear, and so it did. A dove flew in at a window swinging a golden censer in her beak, and the hall was filled with the most delicious smell in the world, and on the tables appeared every meat and drink that each person liked best. This was followed by the appearance of a young girl, bearing in her hands a golden vessel. Immediately Pelles, the Keeper of the Hallows, knelt down, and so did every one in the hall. They prayed, and after a time the girl and the holy vessel vanished.

Every one got up.

'Jesu!' said Sir Lancelot, 'what does all this mean?'

'Sir,' said the King, 'this is the richest thing that any man in the world may have. This is the Holy Sangreal that you have seen here.'

Meanwhile Elaine had been busy. Her lady-in-waiting, Dame Brisen, was an enchantress, and she agreed to help Elaine's plan. She put a spell on Sir Lancelot and gave him a magic cup of wine after dinner which made him do all she wanted. That night Sir Lancelot married Elaine, knowing nothing of what he did. They went to bed in a room of which every window had been blocked to keep out any ray of light, for the enchantment only worked in the dark.

In the morning Sir Lancelot awoke, and not liking to sleep in a room without a breath of air got up and opened the window. As he did so the spell was broken. He turned from the window and saw to his amazement a woman, Elaine, in the room with him. When she told him what she had done, and he thought of the Queen, despair and shame swept over him. He believed that his strength in arms came from his being true to his vows of service to the King and fidelity to the Queen. Now he saw that he had broken his vow and lost both his love and the secret of his strength. 'Alas, that I have lived so long,' he said. He seized his sword and would have killed her, but long habits of the good life stopped him. Elaine swore to him that she had done it because she loved him and would love him till she died. Even in his broken-hearted misery Lancelot respected that, and 'took his leave mildly from the young Lady Elaine.' In sick silence he dressed and armed and rode away as fast as he could.

He went back to the court and was hardly able to meet the eyes of the Queen. No word of this adventure had reached the court, and fortunately there was the bustle of a new campaign in preparation by the King. Sir Lancelot took up his work and avoided the company of the ladies, spending his days in the tilt-yard supervising the training of knights, or at the armourer's inspecting equipment. But the preparations took a long time, and one day a rumour reached court that the daughter of Pelles of Carbonek had had a son whom she said was Lancelot's, and had christened him by Sir Lancelot's first name, Galahad.

Queen Guenevere heard it. She thought of Lancelot's

vows, and his favoured position at court as the friend of the King and the true knight of the Queen. She remembered how unlike himself he had been when he came back to court, and how little she had seen of him all the winter. Black rage came over her. She sent for him, and by the look on the messenger's face Sir Lancelot knew that trouble was coming, and guessed the worst. The Queen was waiting for him in her private room, standing rigid and icy. She called Sir Lancelot traitor and false knight and all the things which had been eating out his heart these past months and which he had been hoping to hide from her. To be the father of this child Galahad had cost Sir Lancelot his honour, his self-respect, his very claim to knighthood by keeping his vows, and now the love and good opinion of his Queen. Galahad was to be the best knight in the world, and more than that, the man in whom all men saw the truly good and happy life achieved, and in whose company they themselves were able to achieve it, but in bringing him into existence Sir Lancelot lost all that he loved and honoured.

He explained about the enchantment as well as he could. It sounded very lame, but Guenevere realized that something strange must have happened and that Sir Lancelot was very much distressed. After a long and bitter conversation 'the Queen held Sir Lancelot excused,' but that was all that could be said. Both remained equally unhappy.

At last the King's expedition was ready, and the fleet set sail, carrying Sir Lancelot away to the wars. Time passed, the months ran into years, and at last the army came home. The Queen had forgiven Sir Lancelot and welcomed him back with King Arthur as in the days before Elaine. But he was not to escape his fate. A feast was given to celebrate the return of the knights, and Pelles sent Elaine, not merely as his daughter but as the wife of Sir Lancelot, with

He flung himself out of the bay window in the Queen's room

a hundred attendants on horseback. The King and Queen received her, and Sir Gawaine, the King's nephew, and Sir Tristram, and all the knights of the Round Table except Sir Lancelot. He saw her arrival from a window in a turret, and watched unseen. He saw the lady-in-waiting, Brisen, who had given him the enchanted cup of wine, now leading by the hand the child Galahad. He saw the royal reception which Elaine was given, and he saw the King and Queen speak to Galahad. That night Sir Lancelot was absent from the hall at dinner, and Elaine remained in vain at court, for 'he would not salute her nor speak with her.'

Naturally this created a scandal at court, and all the mean-minded people were busy mischief-making. Soon it was whispered to the Queen that Sir Lancelot was only pretending not to acknowledge Elaine in order to keep in with the King and Queen, but in secret was meeting her and telling her quite a different story. In a weak moment Guenevere believed it. She sent for him, and said: 'You false traitor knight! See that you leave the court, and never dare, false traitor, to come into my sight again.'

At these words Sir Lancelot fell senseless to the ground. When he recovered, his heart broke and his mind's balance gave way. He flung himself out of the bay window in the Queen's room and ran into the wild woods, a madman, and was not healed for two years.

CHAPTER 16

SIR GAWAINE AND THE QUESTION NOT ASKED

TWO signs seem to have always attended on the Holy Grail, a delicious smell and whatever each beholder liked best to eat and drink. The smell was probably, among other things, a symbol of the opposite of decay—good health and abounding life. The food and drink were a symbol of the plentiful satisfaction of every wish that is found in heaven. But the chief importance of the appearance of the cup and lance was that they were particularly connected with the Last Supper and the Crucifixion, and that with their appearances it was felt that Christ was invisibly present.

These appearances were therefore of immense importance. They were longed for by those who followed the way of Christ and King Arthur, with the passion that one feels for the presence of the hero or the person whom one loves best in the whole world.

As far as we can judge, these tokens appeared generally as the result of a single-minded or intense desire. If a man wanted to see them sincerely enough or long enough, his vision now and then sharpened, and he saw heavenly things, which were there at all times but hidden from the dull sight of people usually looking for quite different things. They existed, of course, like the whole of heaven, for their own heavenly life and joy, and not for the pleasure of the person seeing them. But it was also understood that a man might be able to share that heavenly life if he wished, and indeed be able to find complete happiness in his ordinary life only through contact with it. Therefore when the Hallows appeared to any one, it was necessary for him to be more concerned with the purpose of the Grail than with his own feelings about it.

On this point every one seems to have failed. The people who saw the Grail failed to do something they should have done about it. Through all the stories runs the theme of failure. To see the Grail and to adore was not enough. They should have asked a question, such as 'Whom does the Grail serve?' 'What is the meaning of it?' or 'What is it for?' Because they did not do so, but let themselves be overcome by their feelings of awe and delight, eventually the chance to learn more by these appearances was lost, and the heavenly things seem to have felt it necessary to withdraw from sight altogether.

Had men asked the Question, we do not know what would have happened, but we can surmise that they would have found out more about the heavenly things and the power of God of which they were a sign. Men would have learned how to grow closer to heaven, how to use its help to overcome their sins and weaknesses and to live good lives. The powers of heaven could have moved naturally and happily among them; each man would have been truly a brother to his fellows, and Britain would have become indeed a holy land.

No other country has this legend of the Holy Grail. It was to Britain that Jesus came, and to Britain that Joseph of Arimathea brought the Holy Grail, and in Britain that the life of heaven for a time openly approached the life of earth. It is this approach, this appearance of heavenly things, and the failure to behave rightly towards them, that the famous history of Britain under King Arthur is really about. The fighting and the courage, the ladies and love affairs, the

King and the knightly vows, are all part of the life which arose out of this.

We first hear of the failure to ask the Question in the *High History of the Holy Grail.* It was Midsummer Day, and St. John the Baptist's Day, and King Arthur was holding his court with high ceremony. They were at dinner with a hundred and five knights in hall, when three damsels entered the great chamber. The first two rode on white mules and were splendidly dressed. The first damsel wore a hat because she was quite bald, and had her arm in a sling. The second damsel had a little greyhound on the mule behind her, and a shield slung round her neck, banded with blue and silver with a red cross. Behind them came the most beautiful of all three, on foot, and carrying a whip with which she beat the mules.

The leading damsel explained. They were sent by Pelles, the Keeper of the Hallows. The wound given him by Sir Balin in the dolorous blow had never healed. Now he had 'fallen into a grievous languishment through one that harboured in his hostel, to whom the most Holy Grail appeared. And, because he would not ask the meaning thereof, all the lands were moved to war, and never thereafter might knight meet other but he should fight with him in arms without any reason.' The damsel added that the recent falling off in zeal and achievements by the knights of the Round Table, which had been causing the King much concern, was a result of this. The life of men had been thrown out of gear. She herself became bald at the same time and would remain so until someone asked the Question and so restored the ability of man to live rightly with heavenly powers, or 'achieved the Grail,' a phrase which no one understood then but which was explained later. The damsels then departed.

On their way they met Sir Gawaine. He was the most

magnificent man at court, a different type of man from Sir Lancelot, more fierce and ambitious, proud of his position as King Arthur's nephew, brave and true to his knightly vows. To this splendid and princely knight the damsels offered the chance to seek the Holy Grail, to ask the Question, and to restore the way to a good life in man.

'Damsel,' said Sir Gawaine, 'God grant me courage and will herein that I may come to do this thing according to your wish, whereof I may win honour both of God and of the world.'

They rode for some way together and Sir Gawaine fought battles for the damsels, and they parted company.

As they turned to go the damsel on foot cried out: 'Sir, you are not so heedful as I supposed. You have never asked of my damsel why she carried her arm slung at her neck in this golden stole. And no greater heed will you take at the court of the rich Pelles.'

The other damsel answered: 'Blame not Sir Gawaine only but King Arthur before him, and all the knights that were in the court. For not one of them all that were there was so heedful as to ask me.'

Sir Gawaine rode away at a great pace, but 'sore abashed is he of what the damsel said to him.' On his journey he learned that the knight who had failed to ask the Question was Sir Percivale, and that the land had fallen into such evil ways that Pelles was actually being threatened with siege by a neighbouring lord to gain possession of the Holy Grail and lance.

After many adventures he reached the boundaries of the lands of Pelles. But here he was told that he could not enter unless he brought with him the sword that had beheaded John the Baptist, which was in the possession of King Gurgulain, who did not believe in God but was evil and cruel. If Sir Gawaine could capture the sword and bring it to the castle of the Hallows, it would be known that he was worthy to behold the Holy Grail. And again he was warned not to forget to ask the Question.

So away he went on another long and dangerous quest. On it his faith not only in himself but also in God was severely tested and proved sound, as well as his loyalty to his vows as a Christian knight. Finally he won his way into the castle of Gurgulain and was given the sacred sword. Every day at noon the blade turned bloody, for at that hour John the Baptist was beheaded. As the hour passed, the blade became as clear as emerald, and as green, for that was its colour, the like of which Sir Gawaine had never seen before. Besides winning the sword, he caused Gurgulain to be converted and baptized.

At last he stood again before the castle of Pelles in Carbonek and was allowed to enter. Before him were three deep rushing rivers, one beyond the other, and beyond them all was the inner hold of the castle. Each river was spanned by a single bridge. The first was a bowshot across, and only a foot wide. Neither horse nor man could keep a footing on its narrow thread above the roaring water. As Sir Gawaine paused, a knight called to him to hasten.

'Fair sir,' he answered. 'Teach me how I may pass thereby.'

'Indeed, Sir Knight, I know no other passage to this entrance but this, and if you desire to come to the castle, pass on without fear.'

Sir Gawaine remembered that he had confessed his sins and need not fear to die, and was ashamed that at this last stage he had shown hesitation. He commended himself to God like one who is about to die, and spurred his horse at the plank. As the ravine yawned below him, the bridge became wide and safe. With beating heart Sir Gawaine rode over.

The next bridge was of ice, feeble and thin, and a great height above the water. He surveyed it with the utmost doubt, but did not hesitate to attempt it, and even as his horse's hoofs sounded hollow on it, he found it broad and strong like the other. So with the third, and at last he rode through the inner gate and dismounted at the door of the great hall.

He leaned his shield and spear against the wall and entered unarmed. The hall was empty, painted with pictures and finely furnished. Although outside the light was fading, inside there was a pure brightness without any candles or means of lighting. In the middle of the hall was a magnificent couch beside a chess-board, of which the pieces were of silver and gold. Two knights appeared and made him welcome, bringing him water in golden basins and rich robes of silk and cloth of gold.

Then, taking the sword of John the Baptist, he was led to the chamber of Pelles.

The King lay on a bed hung from the roof by cords running through ivory pulleys. Furs and silks covered him and he had at the corners of his pillow four stones which gave out light; opposite him was a copper pillar on which sat an eagle which held a gold cross in which was set a piece of the true Cross on which Christ had been nailed. Around the bed stood four huge candlesticks in which the attendants kept fresh candles burning.

Sir Gawaine gave courteous greetings, and proffered the sword. Pelles took it and kissed it, with great joy. He told Sir Gawaine that the brightness within the castle came from God because of him, for every time a good knight came to lodge the light appeared. He implored Sir Gawaine that if he should be granted the sight of the Holy Grail he should not fail to ask the Question, and to restore the land to prosperity and health.

Then Sir Gawaine was led away to dinner. He found the hall splendidly furnished, and twelve knights awaiting him. The table was of solid ivory, and on it was venison and wild boar's meat and countless dishes. The vessels were of silver, and the big drinking cups were gold, with carved lids heavy with precious stones; huge candlesticks stood behind each guest and lesser ones upon the table, though their light was lost in the pure serenity which shone throughout the castle.

As they ate the miracle began. Two damsels came down the hall, one carrying the Holy Grail and one the lance whose point bled into the holy cup. They came slowly in front of Sir Gawaine, and the hall was filled with the most sweet smell which always accompanied the Hallows. Gawaine sat motionless, not eating, not speaking. He saw the cup, he saw the point of the lance, and the red blood dripping into the cup, and he saw two angels carrying two gold candlesticks with burning candles. So great a joy filled him that he thought of nothing else. The vision moved on and went into a chapel at the side of the hall. The twelve knights were all downcast, and looked in a stricken manner at Sir Gawaine. Then the damsels appeared again, and came again before him. It seemed to him this time that a third came with them, for in the midst of the Grail he could discern the form of a child. He still sat speechless and overcome. The leader of the knights beckoned to him to speak. Sir Gawaine saw three drops of blood fall on the table. He gazed at them, overcome with awe, and could speak no word.

Then the vision withdrew. The knights looked at one another in despair. But Sir Gawaine could not take his eyes off the three drops of blood which remained. He got up to kiss them, but before he could touch them with hand or lip they vanished away. Again the vision returned, and this time as he looked up he saw above the Grail a figure in the air, a King crowned, nailed on a cross, and a spear fast in His side. Sir Gawaine's heart was rent at the sight, and he remembered nothing but the pain that his King was suffering. He did not hear the leader of the knights call on him by name at this last chance to ask the Question. He could do nothing but gaze, and worship, sitting silent and unheeding.

For the last time the damsels retired into the chapel. The knights signed to the servants to remove the tables, and they all rose and went out, leaving Sir Gawaine alone. He looked round and saw all the doors shut fast. At the end of the long room two candlesticks set with many candles were burning round the chess-board. He walked down to the board. One set of chess-men were silver and one were gold. He sat down at the game, and the gold set played against him, and mated him twice. At the third time, when he hoped to win his revenge, they beat him again, and he swept the pieces off the board.

Sick at heart, he laid himself down on the couch, worn out with his journeys and experiences, and the failure to which they had brought him. He slept on the couch until morning, and at daybreak he went out, found his horse, and rode away.

CHAPTER 17

THE COMING OF GALAHAD TO COURT

IT was twenty years since the founding of the Round Table. All that time the Siege Perilous had stood empty. Sir Lancelot sat on one side of it and different knights at different times on the other. Now, unknown to any one, the day and the knight for whom it was made were due.

On the vigil of Pentecost (which means the day before Whitsunday) the whole court and the knights of the Round Table were gathered at the great feast. As they assembled in the hall for dinner, a lady came riding fast on a lathered horse. She hurried into the hall and went straight to the King and asked for Sir Lancelot. She said she came from Pelles, lord of Carbonek, and must ask him to come with her into a forest. Sir Lancelot's dark eyes rested long on the lady's face. He remembered Carbonek, and Elaine, and the enchanted cup of wine. Was it another trick?

'What do you want me to come for?' he asked.

'You will know when you get there,' she answered. It was not the inviting kind of answer which a deceiving person would make up.

'Well,' he said slowly, 'I will come with you.'

While he was getting ready, people ran to tell the Queen that he was going to see Elaine again. But the Queen was wiser now than in the days when scandalous tongues could make her believe ill of Sir Lancelot. The love between them now was sure and safe from mischief. He came to take leave of her, and promised to be back by dinner-time on the feast day to-morrow. Then he rode away with his squire and the lady.

They rode fast through a forest, and came to an abbey. A squire was waiting, the gates were opened, and in they rode. A great company of nuns came to greet them and made Sir Lancelot welcome. He realized that some strange event must be impending for a man thus to be received into an abbey of nuns. He had not long to wait. As soon as he was unarmed, twelve nuns came in, and with them a young lad of about fifteen, the most beautiful and winning lad that Sir Lancelot had ever seen. In his eyes was a look of natural truth and affection, and he carried himself easily and simply. The nuns brought the youth to Sir Lancelot, and said that he was Galahad. His father stood amazed, but with a deep joy. He exchanged greetings with his son while all the nuns wept. 'Sir,' they said, 'we bring you here this child whom we have cherished, and we pray you to make him a knight, for there is no more worthy man in the world from whom he could receive the order of knighthood.'

'Does he wish this himself?' asked Sir Lancelot.

Galahad and the nuns answered: 'Yes.'

'Then he shall receive the order of knighthood on the high feast.'

So when midnight was passed the whole sisterhood gathered in the chapel, and at the first hour of Whitsunday by the light of a hundred candles Sir Lancelot gave his son that order of knighthood of which he had felt himself robbed by the birth of the boy. He had been tricked into marrying Elaine and so breaking his knightly vow to be true to the Queen. Now he knew that he had moved on into a deeper state where good came out of evil. As Galahad knelt at the altar step before him, Sir Lancelot felt nothing but love for him and for his birth and for the agonies of madness and loss that he himself had thereby suffered. It was the first of those states of love which Galahad was meant to bring about in the world.

That morning Sir Lancelot kept his promise to the Queen and returned to Camelot for the feast. As the knights took their seats at the Round Table there was a stir of excitement, for new golden letters shone round the Siege Perilous. They read: 'Four hundred winter and four and fifty accomplished after the Passion of Our Lord Jesus Christ ought this siege to be fulfilled.' A staggering thought struck Sir Lancelot. Could it be that his son Galahad was the mysterious figure for whom the Siege Perilous had been waiting all these years? 'In the name of God!' he exclaimed, and then said no more. He would wait and see. But he counted up the years reckoned in the new writing round the chair and then said: 'It strikes me that the siege ought to be filled this very day, for this is the Pentecost after the four hundred and fifty-fourth year. And I suggest, if you all agree, that this writing should be covered up until the man comes who will fulfil all this.' So they threw a silk cloth over the seat and hid the writing.

Then the King gave word for dinner. But just as he was going to seat himself a squire came running in and knelt before him and said: 'Sire, down there by the river there is a great stone floating on the water, and I saw a sword sticking up out of it!' A stone, and a sword! King Arthur remembered the sword in the stone which twenty years ago had given him his throne. Pushing back his chair he rose and threw his mantle over his shoulder.

'I will see this marvel,' he said, and went down from the dais and through the hall out on to the steps and down the castle walks to the river bank. Every one in the hall followed in a long procession.

On the water was floating a block of red marble, and out of it rose a fine sword, with a jewelled hilt in which was carved: 'Never shall man take me hence but only he by whose side I ought to hang and he shall be the best knight of the world.'

The King turned to his friend Sir Lancelot, for so long known as the best knight in the world, and clapped him on the shoulder and said that the sword was his.

Sir Lancelot smiled but answered gently: 'Sire, it is not my sword. I am not going to put my hand to it, for I know it is not for me. I am sure that some great thing will begin to-day, such as the adventure of the Holy Grail.'

The King looked round, doubtful whom to call on to attempt the sword. Perhaps Gawaine, his nephew, always trying to rival Sir Lancelot, would have a chance now.

'Fair nephew,' said the King, 'will you try?'

Sir Gawaine looked at Sir Lancelot, and at the sword, and at all the watching faces. He was afraid to fail.

'Sire,' he replied haughtily, 'if you will excuse me, I would rather not.'

King Arthur knew how he longed to be urged. 'Sir, for my sake and at my command, try to take the sword.'

'Sire, at your command I will obey,' answered Gawaine, and stepped on to the bank, a splendid figure in purple and gold, his red hair shining, his face white with excitement. He grasped the sword, but it held fast. Stiff with humiliation, Sir Gawaine stepped back. The King knew that someone else must fail too, to save his nephew's pride. He called on Sir Percivale, who set little store on pride or prestige. He tried and failed, and stepped back smiling. Then the King decided to leave the sword for the moment and to go back to the neglected feast.

They all took their places once more in the hall, and dinner proceeded. Suddenly, with a clap like thunder, all

'By God, fair fellows and lords, we have seen marvels to-day!'

the windows and doors closed. But yet the light did not grow less. There was dead silence, and every heart was afraid.

The voice of the King spoke cheerily. 'By God, fair fellows and lords, we have seen marvels to-day! But before night we shall see greater ones!'

As he spoke there came in an old man dressed in white, unknown to any one in the hall. He led with him a young knight in red armour, with neither shield nor sword but an empty scabbard by his side. Sir Lancelot's heart moved. He had seen the young knight at the first hour of that very day. No one else knew him or had ever seen him before. The old man led him to the King and said: 'Sire, I bring you here a young knight of king's lineage and of the kin of Joseph of Arimathea, by whom the marvels of this court shall be accomplished.'

'Sir,' said the King, standing up, 'you are right welcome, and the young knight with you.'

The old man helped the knight to take off his armour. Under it he wore a tunic of scarlet linen, and the old man hung on his shoulders a cloak edged with ermine. Then he said to the young man: 'Sir, follow me.' He led him to the Round Table, to the Siege Perilous. Every one saw Sir Lancelot in the next seat exchange a greeting with the stranger. The old man lifted up the silk cloth, and the writing round the chair had changed to: 'This is the siege of Sir Galahad the High Prince.'

'Sir,' said the old man, 'that place is yours.'

In dead silence the young knight sat down. Sir Lancelot drew a sharp breath. Nothing happened; the lad sat easily, looking round him quite naturally at the faces of famous knights. Then he turned and said good-bye to the old man, who left the hall. Every one began to talk again, and dinner went on. But now the news was buzzing round that the name of the new knight was Galahad and so he must be Sir Lancelot's son. The old story was revived of Sir Lancelot and the tricked marriage with Elaine of Carbonek. People slipped out of the hall and ran to the Queen's apartments with the news, and swore the newcomer was exactly like Sir Lancelot. The Queen answered: 'I should like to see him; he must be a noble man, for so is his father.'

After dinner the King took Sir Galahad down to the river to see the sword in the marble rock. The Queen saw the company going out, and she gathered her ladies and went too. The King told Sir Galahad what an extraordinary thing it was and how several famous knights had failed to draw the sword.

Sir Galahad looked surprised. 'Sire, it is not extraordinary,' he answered politely, 'because the adventure is not theirs, but mine. I knew this sword would be here, so I did not bring one, but here is the scabbard.' It was indeed the scabbard which Merlin had left on the island accessible only by a bridge of six inches width. No one knew how Galahad had won it, and he said no more about it. Galahad took hold of the hilt and drew the sword out as easily as the young lad Arthur had done twenty years ago in a London churchyard. He slid it into the scabbard, and said smiling: 'It is better there than in the stone.' Then he took it out again and looked it up and down admiringly. 'It is the sword of Sir Balin the Savage, the great fighter,' he said proudly. 'With it he killed his brother Sir Balan by mistake.' He went on to tell the King the story and the King smiled at Sir Lancelot, for they had known of the events he spoke of before Sir Galahad was ever born.

A lady came riding on a white horse towards them. She asked the King and Queen if Sir Lancelot was there, and then said to him weeping: 'Ah, Sir Lancelot, how your reputation is changed even since this morning.'

'Damsel, what do you mean?' asked Sir Lancelot, undisturbed.

'Only this morning you were the best knight in the world. But who should say so now would be a liar, for there is now one better than you, and it is proved by the adventure of the sword.'

But Sir Lancelot answered: 'As for that, I know quite well I never was the best.'

'Yes you were,' replied the lady, 'and you are still, of all ordinary men in the world.' Then she turned to the King and told him that because the Holy Grail appeared in his kingdom and his house, he had the greatest honour that would ever befall any king of Britain.

Soon the King was busy arranging for a tournament to be held that afternoon in the town meadow. Every one wanted to see how Sir Galahad would fight, and Sir Lancelot himself was eager to see him do well. He did indeed do well, breaking many spears and coming to no harm himself. By the end of the afternoon he had worsted every knight he had met except Sir Lancelot and Sir Percivale. But the adventures of the day were not yet over.

CHAPTER 18

HOW THE QUEST BEGAN

AS the shadows began to creep from the elms across the meadow on the long June evening, the whole company turned back to the town and followed the King to evensong in the cathedral. After that they went to supper, every knight sitting in his place. Sir Lancelot discussed the day's sport with all the knights and Sir Galahad.

Suddenly there was a terrific peal of thunder. A beam of light seven times more bright than sunlight slid into the hall, and filled the whole place with brilliance. Each knight looked at his neighbour, and found that in this light he appeared much pleasanter than he had ever been before. So great an awe filled each man that nobody could speak, and they all sat stone still.

Down the beam of light glided the Holy Grail, a cup covered in white samite so that no one could see it, nor could they see if any one carried it. Once again the bounties of the Grail were displayed, the exquisite smell, the food and drink that delighted each man most. Through the length of the hall went the holy vessel and then vanished.

After a while the power of speech returned, and the King gave thanks to God for His good grace that He had shown them all on this feast of Pentecost. But thanks and humility were not enough for Sir Gawaine. He struck the table and stood up. 'We have had whatever we desired to eat and drink,' he declared stormily, 'but one thing we were denied, that we did not see the Holy Grail because it was so completely covered. So, I here make a vow that to-morrow, without delay, I shall set out on a Quest of the Holy Grail, and that I shall keep it up a year and a day if need be, and I will never return to court till I have seen it more openly than it was shown here.'

There were shouts of agreement, and one by one the knights rose and took the same oath. Sir Lancelot knew that the motive was wrong, as it was rejecting the decision of God not to show the holy thing openly to their eyes, but he also knew that the whole day had been leading up to this, and the roots of it all lay far, far back and were not for him to disentangle or deny. So he too took the vow.

As knight after knight pledged himself, King Arthur foresaw the break-up of the Round Table, the scattering of its members, and the ruin of its work in the kingdom; he foresaw all the force on the side of law and religion leaving Britain on this Quest, and the evil so hardly trampled down rearing itself again, and himself old and with no band of young men to live well and fight for the right. Tears were in his eyes as he faced his nephew. 'Alas! You have killed me by this vow,' he said, 'for you have broken the most glorious and truest order of knighthood that was ever seen in any kingdom of the world. When they leave here I know that they will never meet again, for many will die on this Quest. I regret it very deeply, for I have loved them as my life. The scattering of this fellowship breaks my heart, for it is a long time now that we have been together. Gawaine, Gawaine, you have brought great sorrow to me, for I think that my true fellowship will never meet here again.'

'Ah, Sire,' said Sir Lancelot, 'comfort yourself. It will be a great honour to us, and much more than if we died in any other pursuit, and we are bound to die some time.'

'Lancelot!' The King turned and looked at him. 'The very love I have had for you all my life makes me so sad. For there was never a Christian king who had so many worthy men as I have had to-day at the Round Table, and that is the cause of my grief.'

The King was not to be comforted, and he was joined in his foreboding by the Queen and all the court. Every woman wept and every man felt that a time of greatness was coming to an end. The whole town was stirred by the news and with preparations for so many departures, and with so many farewells. The Queen sent for Galahad and had a few words with him in case she never saw him again.

At last the time came for bed, though no one could rest. The King ordered that the High Prince Galahad should sleep in the royal bed that night and be lodged like a king. After a restless night King Arthur went early to Sir Lancelot's rooms and asked him if there were any possible means of stopping the Quest. But one of the chief oaths of a knight was to be true to his promise, and this Lancelot pointed out. They both stood silent and knew that the thing must run its course. Sir Lancelot put his hand on the King's shoulder, and so they stood a moment, these two close friends of twenty years or more, who had at all times been each other's first and chief support. Then they went together to join the Queen at an early celebration of the Eucharist to mark the opening of the Quest.

After the service a hundred and fifty knights, the whole of the Round Table, took leave of the King and Queen.

A long procession of knights wound through the streets to the gate, followed by cheering and weeping townspeople. The King rode with his knights for the last time, and found Sir Lancelot beside him as he rode. Neither spoke, for the King's heart was too full for speech.

The gate was reached, and the King drew rein. Out rode his fellowship of knights, the most glorious band of men in any kingdom, famous throughout Christendom for courage and honour. Each one saluted the King who had created the knighthood which had made them more than other men, and who had at all times been their true head. Then one by one they spurred their horses and rode away.

CHAPTER 19

SIR GAWAINE ON THE QUEST

SIR GAWAINE meant well when he started on the Grail Quest. He was proud and impatient, jealous and hot-tempered, but he was not a cruel or wicked man. If the Quest had brought what he thought was a good life, plenty of fighting, action, and adventure, he would have done well, whatever hardships or dangers he had to put up with. But nothing like that happened.

He set off in hot spirits, determined to dare any dangers for the sake of the Grail. He rode all day and met no one. All next day and the day after he met no one. He rode across country but met only silent woods and deserted paths. He began to be depressed and irritated. At last he saw roofs and hurried there. It was an abbey, and the monks told him that Sir Galahad had recently been there, and they showed him the way he had gone. Sir Gawaine spurred after him. He came to another abbey and there they told him of all kinds of adventures which had happened to Sir Galahad. Sir Gawaine was angry, jealous of the new knight who sat in the Perilous Siege and had been acclaimed the High Prince. How foolish he had been not to go with Sir Galahad when they all separated! He might have known that the adventures would be all reserved for him.

As he was dismounting, sullen and disappointed, one of the monks guessed his thoughts and remarked that even if he caught up with Sir Galahad they would not be likely to stay together long as Sir Gawaine was full of unpleasantness and Sir Galahad was not. This annoyed him very much, but he was cheered by the unexpected arrival of Sir Gareth, his youngest brother, with whom he was at least able to talk about things of the court, which livened his boredom.

Next morning they attended the Eucharist, and rode off together. They met Sir Uwaine le Avoutre, who had also had no adventures at all, and they all three agreed to keep together, which was not the original idea of the Quest. That day they passed near the Castle of Maidens, where seven knights were on patrol. They had no quarrel with them, and they were supposed to be sworn to a holy Quest, on which it was plain that no unnecessary killing should be done, but they were so bored that they not only fought the seven but killed them all, which was quite unnecessary.

They felt guilty about this, and decided to separate after all. Sir Gawaine came at evening to a hermitage and asked for shelter for the night. 'I am a knight of King Arthur who is on the Quest of the Holy Grail, and my name is Gawaine.'

The hermit looked at him and saw right into his heart in the disconcerting way of people whose minds are filled with the clearness which the love of God brings.

'Sir,' he answered gravely, 'I would rather know how things are between you and God.'

'I am quite willing to tell you all about my life if you want me to,' answered Sir Gawaine, and so he did.

The hermit thought very little of the story, and when Sir Gawaine finished by describing his battle of three against seven, the hermit said that Sir Galahad had beaten and unhorsed the seven but had refrained from killing them. He said that Sir Gawaine would get nowhere by going on in this spirit, and he must start all over again. 'You must make amends for this killing,' he said.

Sir Gawaine became extremely haughty. 'Sir, what penance shall I do?' he asked.

'I will think it out, and tell you.'

'You will do no such thing,' replied Sir Gawaine. 'It is quite impossible for us knights on adventures to do penance; we have enough to put up with in the trials and hardships we have to undergo.'

'Very well,' said the hermit, and said no more.

Next morning the knight left as early as he could. He met Sir Aglavale and Sir Griflet and rode with them for four days with no success, and on the fifth they separated. All the summer he searched England for adventures, from Whitsun to Michaelmas, and he was thoroughly frustrated. He met Sir Ector, who said that he had met twenty knights who all complained of the same thing.

'I wonder where that brother of yours, Sir Lancelot, is,' said Gawaine. Wherever Sir Lancelot was, things were certain to be happening.

'I have not heard a word of him,' said Sir Ector, 'nor of Sir Galahad, Sir Percivale, or Sir Bors.'

'Well, if they cannot find the Grail, it is a waste of time for the rest of us to try.'

One Saturday evening in October, wet and rough, with darkness coming down early, they came to a ruined chapel by the side of the track. Although most of the roof had gone there was one bit which would keep the rain out, so they decided to spend the night there. They alighted and took off their saddle-bags containing their provisions, and made themselves as comfortable as they could. They talked awhile, wondering where they were and how much longer it would all go on. Then they fell asleep, and both of them dreamed a dream.

Sir Gawaine dreamed that he went into a field rich with good grass and flowers. In it was a herd of bulls, a hundred and fifty black and three white. The white were feeding and the black were not, but looked restless and uneasy. They all said: 'Let us go and look for a better pasture than this,' and when they began to move out of the field he saw they were so thin and weak that they could hardly stand. The three white ones went too. After a time some came back, but only one white one. When that one came back, a great commotion broke out among the black ones about the lack of food, and they all scattered and disappeared.

Sir Ector's dream was that he and Sir Lancelot, his brother, took two horses and said to each other: 'Let us go and seek what we shall not find.' Then a man came and beat Sir Lancelot and took away his armour and made him put on a rough garment full of knots, and get on to a donkey. He and Sir Ector rode so until they came to a well, and both had a violent desire to drink. When Sir Lancelot stooped to drink, the water sank so that he could not reach it. He got up and went back the way he had come. Sir Ector went on till he came to a rich man's house where they were having a wedding, but the rich man said: 'Sir Knight, there is no room for you here.'

When they both awoke, Sir Gawaine and Sir Ector told each other their dreams and pondered over them.

'I shall not feel happy until I get some news of Lancelot,' said Sir Ector gloomily.

As they sat talking in the dark, suddenly they clutched each other, for there floated in the air in front of them a candle, clear and steady, held by a hand and forearm, covered in red samite, with a crude bridle over the arm. The hand carried the candle past them and disappeared among the chapel ruins. A voice said: 'Knights, full of bad faith and feeble intention, these two things have failed you, and so you may not come to the adventure of the Holy Grail.'

See p. 136

There floated in front of them a candle, clear and steady

When they had recovered from their shock, Sir Gawaine said: 'Sir Ector, did you hear what I heard?'

'Yes, indeed,' answered Sir Ector, 'I heard it all. We had better go and find a hermit to explain it, because it seems to me we are doing all this for nothing.'

Next morning they rode on. In a valley they met a knight, correctly armed like themselves, who used the proper salutes and gestures, and offered to joust with them. Sir Gawaine eagerly accepted the challenge. At the first charge his spear went right through the stranger's breast and came out at the back. When Sir Gawaine bent over him he spoke muffled through his helm.

'I am as good as dead. I am of King Arthur's court, and was a fellow of the Round Table, and we were sworn friends. I am Sir Uwaine le Avoutre, and I was on the Quest of the Holy Grail. May God forgive you, for every one will say one sworn brother knight has killed another.' Off came his helm, and Sir Gawaine saw that it was true.

'Alas, that this should happen to me!' he exclaimed in despair, not thinking how eagerly he had accepted the joust.

'Well,' said Sir Uwaine, 'since I am going to die this way I could not die at the hands of a more famous fighter. But when you get back to court, commend me to my lord Arthur, and to all those who are still alive. And for brotherhood think of me.' And so he died.

After this Sir Gawaine had no more heart for the Quest which had turned out so drearily and ended for him so disastrously. He and Sir Ector found a hermit who explained their dreams and the vision. The herd of bulls were the Round Table, and the good grass and flowers were humility and patience which are always fresh and green, and in which people said the Round Table had been founded.

But the black bulls were too proud and discontented to feed on the pasture. The white ones were Sir Percivale, Sir Bors, and Sir Galahad. The search for better pasture was the Quest of the Grail, undertaken by most without humility or patience or even admission of their sins. Of the three chosen knights only one would return.

In Sir Ector's dream, the Holy Grail was that which they could not find. But Sir Lancelot abandoned his pride and took on humility, wearing poor clothes and riding Christ's beast, a donkey. The well was the grace of God, and when he saw that he could not reach it he went back and was ready to start all over again.

The candle was the good life in Christ, the hand the Holy Ghost, and the bridle was the control of oneself. The clearness of the good life, the love of the Holy Ghost, and the effort to control one's own will had failed in these two knights. They listened glumly. Sir Gawaine asked why on this Quest as on no other they had met with no events at all. The hermit said that their hearts were full of self-will and importance, and the Holy Grail withdrew from wherever they went, and from people like them.

'Sir, in that case it is quite useless for us to go on in the Quest.'

The hermit answered: 'That is so. There are a hundred or more like you who will get nothing out of it but dishonour.'

So Sir Gawaine and Sir Ector inquired in what direction lay Camelot, and turned their horses thither.

CHAPTER 20

SIR BORS

SIR GAWAINE had seen in his dream three white bulls which were the three knights who succeeded in the Quest of the Grail. These three knights were Sir Bors, Sir Percivale, and Sir Galahad, and the only one to return from the Quest was Sir Bors.

He was the nephew of Sir Lancelot, and like him came from Benwick, or Bayonne, on the Atlantic coast of southern France. His full name was Sir Bors de Ganis. To him the things like the Hallows that were to others only fancies or remote beliefs were as real as horses and armour. He was a strong and skilful knight, but unlike most of his friends he lived as much in the spiritual world as in the courtly and earthly. At all times his chief earthly devotion was to Sir Lancelot, through whom he learned devotion also to King Arthur and, though he was sometimes angry with her, to the Queen.

In the first adventure in which we meet Sir Bors, long before the Grail Quest, he saw the Holy Grail. He came to Carbonek, the castle of the Hallows. Pelles lived there, with his daughter Elaine and her son Galahad. As soon as Sir Bors sat down to dinner the Holy Grail appeared, attended by a white dove, with a little gold censer in her beak, and a maiden, and there appeared on the tables each man's choice of food and drink.

Every one knelt down at the sight of the heavenly things, and the room was filled with the sweetest smell in all the world. They prayed, and the dove and the maiden and the

Grail vanished. Sir Bors determined not to be in haste to leave the castle where such things happened. 'I will lie in this castle this night,' he said. King Pelles warned him that many people injured themselves by pressing for adventures for which they were not fit. But Sir Bors was not presumptuous; he was single-hearted, and he knew what he wanted to follow. He confessed his sins and received absolution before retiring to bed for the night.

He was led into a fine large bedroom, with many doors. He sent every one away and lay down fully armed on the bed. Suddenly he saw a light, and a mighty spear with a flaming point was flung by an invisible hand into the room and smote him on the shoulder. As he sprang up it vanished, and after a while he lay down again, in much pain from his wound. He was hardly on the bed when a knight came in, armed and carrying his sword.

'Arise, Sir Knight,' said the stranger, 'and fight with me.'

'I am badly hurt,' said Sir Bors, 'but yet I shall not fail you.'

They fought together a long time, until at last Sir Bors smote him down and the knight yielded.

Again Sir Bors lay down to rest. But now an uproar arose in his room, and a whistling of countless arrows and clicking of bowstrings. Arrows struck him on every side, glancing off his armour or piercing him where he was not protected. In the middle of the uproar a hideous lion rushed at him from he knew not where. It knocked his shield out of his hand, but Sir Bors swung his sword and cut off its head. In a moment its place was taken by a dragon, the emblem of King Arthur, and in its forehead were letters of gold that seemed to Sir Bors to mean the King. A leopard followed, and fought with Sir Bors. The dragon spat out of its mouth a hundred small dragons which immediately killed the old dragon and tore it to pieces.

Then an old man came into the room, and sat down in a fine chair, and round his neck were two adders. The old man had a harp, and he sang a song about how Joseph of Arimathea came into this land of Britain. When he had ended he turned to Sir Bors and told him to leave the castle. 'For here you shall have no more adventures; and full honourably have you done, and better shall you do hereafter.' Then again Sir Bors saw the snow-white dove with the little golden censer in her beak, and instantly the clamour and tempest in the room ceased, and the exquisite smell filled the air.

In the stillness there came in four children carrying tapers, surrounding an old man who had a censer in one hand and a spear of vengeance in the other. The old man told Sir Bors to go and look for Sir Lancelot and tell him these events, and urge him to attempt to gain in the spiritual life the manhood and prowess he had in earthly life, in which he surpassed every other person. Four fair women came by, and Sir Bors saw them pass into a room 'where was great light as it were a summer light.' The women knelt down before an altar of silver with four pillars, and a figure like a bishop knelt with them. Sir Bors saw in the air above the bishop's head a silver sword, and the brightness of it dazzled him. As he stared, half blinded, a voice said: 'Go hence, Sir Bors, for as yet you are not worthy to be in this place.' So he drew back from the door and returned to his bed till morning.

The next day he took his horse and rode away to Camelot and told Sir Lancelot all that had happened.

'Better shall you do hereafter,' the old man had said, and in Sir Bors's Quest of the Grail those words came true. Soon after he had ridden out from Camelot and parted from the other knights he met a holy man who warned him that no one could achieve the Grail if he was hiding evil longings in his heart, and that strict discipline was needed by any one who hoped to succeed. At the next hermitage Sir Bors confessed his sins in preparation for the Quest. The holy man told him to eat nothing but bread and water until he should 'sit at the table where the Sangreal shall be.'

Sir Bors agreed, and asked how the hermit knew that he would sit there.

'I know it,' said the holy man; 'but there will be but few of your fellows with you.'

'All is welcome,' said Sir Bors, 'that God sends.'

The hermit gave him a scarlet coat to wear instead of his shirt under his armour until he had found the Holy Grail.

He had many adventures, and strange sights appeared to him and strange tests were made of his constancy in following the Quest. He met two knights who had captured his brother Lionel and were leading him away tied naked on a horse, and were beating him with thorns. Sir Lionel never spoke a word. As Sir Bors was rushing to his rescue he heard a cry for help in the name of Christ's mother Mary, and saw a knight assaulting a girl in the bushes. It was a desperate dilemma for him, because he could only help one of the two victims. He cried: 'Fair sweet Lord Jesu Christ, whose sworn man I am, keep Lionel, my brother, and for Mary's sake I will help this maiden.'

He rescued the girl and then rode off at full speed to find his brother. But an enchantment was put on him, and he found a dead body which he thought was Lionel's. He carried it to a ruined chapel and laid it on a tomb of marble, and mourned that his brother's death was the result of his own decision.

Another equally bad dilemma awaited him. He had

Then he took his arms and his horse and rode away

sworn to give his love to no woman until he had achieved this Quest of the Grail. Now he met a priest in the forest who told him that he was coming to a castle where a beautiful young woman lived who had loved him for a long time and would die if he did not give her his love, but that if he did his Uncle Lancelot would die. 'Choose you now the one or the other.'

Sir Bors was taken into a high tower where he found knights and ladies, and music and feasting. As he went in he forgot everything except the pleasures in front of him. He forgot Sir Lionel and Sir Lancelot, and delighted only in the people around him. Then came the most beautiful woman he had ever seen, and the whole gathering declared that she was their lady and that she loved none but Sir Bors. Suddenly everything came back to him and he became extremely ill at ease and did not know how to answer her. To his horror she said that if he did not become her lover she would jump off the battlements of the tower, and that twelve of her ladies would jump with her, and that Sir Bors would cause the death of them all. He was in terrible distress, but he held firm to his vowed singleness in the Quest, and in his heart he knew that he was not responsible for any such desperate action as the ladies declared they would perform. From the top of the tower one lady cried to him to save them. He looked up at them and made no answer. They flung themselves off the edge. In horror he crossed himself, and as he did so there was a yell as if all the fiends in hell were about him, and tower, lady, and gentlewomen all vanished, and so did the chapel in which he had laid what he thought was the body of his brother.

'Fair father God,' said Sir Bors, 'I am grievously escaped.' Then he took his arms and his horse and rode away.

CHAPTER 21

SIR PERCIVALE

WHEN King Arthur was a lad, and all the great names of his time were still unknown, Merlin the wizard spoke a prophecy. He said that two men should come who would have no equal but one in valour and good living, and their names would be Sir Percivale of Wales and Sir Lamorak of Wales.

Years went by and the lads who were young with Arthur grew into men around him, and the first generation of knights, among them Sir Lamorak the Welshman, established order and ruled Britain. Their life was hard and rough, constantly on horseback and in arms. One by one the knights of the Round Table hunted out people who defied the King, and enforced law all over the country. It was a task which took all their time and left them little leisure. If a man was not a fighting man he became a priest or a hermit, who was a solitary holy man, sometimes an ordained priest, but not always. There was little choice besides those two types of life.

As time went on, however, this simple way of living drew to an end. Gradually order became established and the wicked were either killed or made to submit to King Arthur's ideals of justice and law. The next generation of knights found a different kind of world facing them, in which they had to live well in a peaceful life without the stimulus of an enemy.

These young men grew up quite different from their fathers. Thinking and acting rightly were more important to them than fighting. This was very difficult for the older knights to understand. Only the few like King Arthur and Sir Lancelot, who had always tried to think rightly as well as fight bravely, realized that the young ones were as good as the old, and better suited to new times. Most of the older generation simply despised them. When Sir Percivale came to court he seemed another of the new quiet intellectual type. Sir Aglavale brought him, says Sir Thomas Malory, and asked King Arthur to make his young squire a knight. As King Arthur looked at the young man, who was so obviously different from his stalwart elder brother Sir Lamorak, he saw something in him besides the strong arm and quick eye of the fighter, and answered: 'For the love of Sir Lamorak, and for his father's love, he shall be made a knight to-morrow.'

So he was, 'but the King and all the knights thought it would be long before he proved a good knight.' That evening at dinner, when each knight sat below the Round Table at long tables in order of prowess, the King directed Sir Percivale to join the unproved knights at the bottom of the hall. Now among Queen Guenevere's ladies there was one who was dumb. On this particular evening this maiden astonished every one by coming into the hall as if she were following an angel guide. She went through the throng of tables and servers past all the distinguished people until she reached the newly made knight Sir Percivale. She took him by the hand and spoke in a clear voice: 'Arise Sir Percivale, the noble knight and God's knight, and go with me.' He did so, and every eye in the hall watched them. She led him to the Round Table itself, and put him by the seat on the right hand of the Perilous Siege and said: 'Fair knight, take here thy siege, for that siege belongeth to thee and to none other.' She then went straight out of the hall, asked for a priest, confessed her sins, and died. Naturally every one took a great deal more notice of Sir Percivale after this.

It soon became clear that he was an unusual person. He saw visions. He saw old men and lions and children, and all manner of things which he did not always understand, but which made round him a kind of world which was half-way between this world and heaven. He was afraid of nothing. That other world of his seemed to give him freedom from the fears of this one. Gradually he moved more into that other world, in which the spiritual creatures used to become visible, put him to tests, and disappear. Some were good and from heaven; more were evil and from hell. He had not yet won through to a truly heavenly world, and he suffered very greatly in this stage.

He set out with all the Round Table on the Quest of the Holy Grail. One day he was riding with Sir Lancelot, who alone of the elder knights understood the spiritual struggles which in the new generation had replaced the tournament battles of the old. Towards them rode Sir Galahad, who had already gone through Sir Percivale's half-way world into the world on the other side which was sure and clear and heavenly. Sir Lancelot was realizing more and more that the things his son knew were more important than the quests and battles of the other knights, and were the basis of the laws and vows of the King himself. But when he and Sir Percivale met Sir Galahad they did not recognize him because he was disguised. They challenged him, whereupon he charged his father and unhorsed him, and drawing his sword knocked Sir Percivale out of the saddle. A recluse, or religious lady, living a solitary life like a hermit, saw the rare sight of Sir Lancelot unhorsed. She recognized Sir Galahad, who spurred on his horse and rode fast out of sight.

Sir Lancelot rode after him, but Sir Percivale asked the

recluse about the strange knight. She warned him to follow Sir Galahad in love and not in envy or anger.

On his way Sir Percivale was crossing a deep valley at midday, when a party of twenty horsemen came cantering out of a copse towards him, and shouted a challenge, demanding whence he came. 'From the court of King Arthur!' he answered, and a yell came back: 'Slay him!' He went down under a thunder of hoofs and clash of arms. His good horse fell slain, and though it half crushed him it saved him from death by trampling. In a daze, scarcely knowing if it was another vision or actual happening, he saw a knight, in the red armour of Sir Galahad, and heard him shout, and then heard hard riding and the clash and crash of falling men in armour, and shouts of dismay and rough orders to retreat, and still the sound of blows and heavy falls. He crawled out from under his dead horse just in time to see the red knight chasing the remains of the robber party back into the copse. He shouted, but Sir Galahad rode on.

Now Sir Percivale was in a very bad state, for he had no horse. In his armour he could only walk with difficulty and the valley was totally deserted. He sat by the road and waited for someone to pass, but no one had a horse to spare. When it grew dark he went to sleep, and was awoken at midnight by a woman. She called him by his name and asked him fiercely what he was doing. He answered: 'I do neither good nor great ill.'

'If you will promise me to do what I ask some time when I shall call on you, I will lend you my own horse.'

Sir Percivale was so delighted with the idea of a horse to get him away from this desolate spot that he agreed at once. The woman went away and soon came back in the starlight with an immense horse completely harnessed as became a knight's charger. Without waiting Sir Percivale mounted and rode off. As he came out of the valley the moon rose, and the horse put on speed. Faster and faster went the drumming hoofs; hedges, streams, and open commons rushed up and were left behind. Still the pace increased, and Sir Percivale realized that this was no mortal horse, and that he was in the grip of an enchantment. He could not check his steed, but clung to its saddle, and felt the world rush by. In an hour they had travelled four days' journey. Sir Percivale saw a stretch of roaring water coming, and knew that the horse was going to hurl him into it. Quickly he made the sign of the cross on his forehead. The horse gave a ghastly shriek and flung Sir Percivale on the ground. To his horror he saw the animal turn into a fiend that went into the water crying and roaring, and where it went the water burned in a track of fire.

Sir Percivale prayed long and thankfully that night, until the chilly morning crept into the sky. Then he saw that he was on a black mountain-side ringed round by the sea. He began to turn back from the coast, and soon found that there were other dangers than hunger and loneliness. As he was making his way through a rough valley he saw a big snake dragging by the neck a struggling young lion cub. In a moment a full-grown lion came roaring and growling, and began to attack the serpent. Sir Percivale went to the help of the lion, because he was the more natural beast of the two, and killed the snake with a cut of his sword. When the lion saw that he instantly became friendly, and by walking round and rubbing his head against Sir Percivale and purring, he did all that a beast might do to make friends with a man. The knight stroked him on the neck and shoulders and thanked God for the fellowship of the beast. So they stayed and rested all the morning, and when the midday heat came on the lion picked up his cub and carried him away.

Then Sir Percivale was alone in this land to which an evil spell had brought him. He was tempted to despair, but the history says he 'comforted himself in Our Lord Jesus and besought Him that no temptations should bring him out of God's service, but to endure as His true champion.' As soon as he had ended his prayer, the lion came back, and kept him company all day, and couched at his feet when darkness fell, and they slept together. The knight had horrible dreams and awoke shuddering, but found the lion and stroked his tawny back and was reassured by him.

Next day at noon he saw a ship scudding over the sea towards him. As it neared land he hurried down to meet it. He found it was covered in black silk, and in it a lady, most beautiful, dressed in great magnificence. She called him by his name and said she would bring him to Sir Galahad. Sir Percivale was so thankful to be rescued from this dreadful place that he never thought of questioning or proving her. He agreed to do everything she suggested and believed all she told him about how badly she had been treated by her husband. It was very hot, and she called a waiting woman and had a tent pitched on the shore. She sat inside and talked to Sir Percivale. In the course of conversation he made the sign of the cross. Instantly the whole tent rose up in a whirlwind and changed into a thick swirling black cloud. The lady screamed: 'You have betrayed me,' and fled roaring and yelling into the ship, which instantly shot away over the sea leaving a trail of fire.

Sir Percivale was left in a turmoil of shamed and confused thoughts. After a long time he saw a different ship approaching. In it was an old man who talked to him about his narrow escape. 'That lady was the master fiend of hell, which has power over all other devils.' He reminded the knight of his bad dreams, and he realized that he had dreamed of this woman, but that he had been so thankful to be rescued from the mountain-side that he had not cared on what dishonourable terms the rescue was made. The old man warned him to be careful, and vanished.

But the ship remained. So Sir Percivale said good-bye to the lion, took his sword and arms, and went on board, set the sail, and immediately the ship glided away from that grim shore.

CHAPTER 22

THE VOYAGE OF THE THREE KNIGHTS

AFTER Sir Bors's adventure with the ladies on the top of the tower he found his brother Lionel again. But they quarrelled, and Sir Bors was going to draw his sword on him when a voice sounded over them, and a fiery cloud came down between them, scorching them and striking them to the earth. Sir Bors heard a voice say: 'Take your way at once to the sea, for Sir Percivale awaits you there.' He asked his brother's pardon and set out. He slept that night in an abbey and was awoken by a voice urging him to the sea. He got up, armed, went silently to the stables and saddled his horse, and rode out through a broken wall and heard the sound of the sea. A shape glimmered on the water, and he rode his horse down over the sand. It was a ship, but no wood ever glowed with that strange whiteness. The hull was draped with white samite, and the sails were of the same. All was still and silent. A gangway ran down on to the beach. Sir Bors commended himself to Christ and went on board.

As soon as his feet touched the deck, the ship drew out from the shore, but with no sign of crew at work. The night wind whistled past his face, and it seemed to him that the ship was flying, not sailing. He could see nothing, so he lay down and went to sleep. When he awoke he saw a knight, armed but without his helm, and when he turned he recognized Sir Percivale. With great joy they greeted each other, and told how each was brought to that strange meeting. Sir Percivale told Sir Bors how an old man had

See p. 149

He knew that the horse was going to hurl him into the roaring water

Sir Galahad

brought this ship and rescued him from the desolate mountain-side. Each found in the fellowship of the other a strengthening of that better, happier world which more and more they sought in their lives, and felt to be natural to Sir Galahad.

'We lack nothing,' said Sir Percivale, 'except Sir Galahad the good knight.'

In the meantime Sir Galahad was being brought with equal directness to the seashore and the ship. Near Carbonek he was roused, like Sir Bors, at night, by a lady who bade him take horse at once and follow her. Sir Galahad obeyed. The lady led him through the night by unknown ways, until from afar he too heard the sound of the sea. There on the dark shore, in the dimness between night and morning, was a ship. As he came up level with it the voices of Sir Bors and Sir Percivale came across the water: 'Sir Galahad, you are welcome, for we have waited long for you.'

The lady and Sir Galahad left their horses and went on board. The knights greeted each other with great joy, and made the lady welcome, though no one knew her and she gave no name. As the sun rose they sat and told each other all their adventures, and ended with renewed joy to have found each other and to be on the Quest of the Holy Grail once more. Ever faithful to his dearest friend Sir Bors sighed and said: 'Ah, Sir Galahad, if Sir Lancelot, your father, were here, then we should be wholly at ease, for then we should need nothing.'

They came to a dangerous passage between two rocks, where they had to change to another ship. The lady led them on board, where they found neither man nor woman. They walked from end to end, and found an inscription saying: 'Thou man which shalt enter into this ship, beware that thou be in steadfast belief, for I am Faith. And therefore beware how thou enterest unless thou be steadfast, for if thou fail I shall not help you.'

Then the lady turned to Sir Percivale. 'Do you know what I am?' she asked. They all wanted to know.

'No, indeed,' he said. 'To my knowledge I never saw you before.'

'I am your sister,' she replied, 'daughter to King Pellinore, and you are the man that I love most. So if you do not wholly believe in Jesus Christ, on no account come aboard this ship, or you will perish. For He is so complete that He will allow no half-believers within Him.'

Sir Percivale was overjoyed to have found his sister, of whom at many times he had gone in search. She had two names, Blanchefleur and Dindrane, and she was sent now to be the guide and teacher of the three knights.

In the ship were many marvels, among them a sword which made its owner unable to be wounded or to become weary, and three spindles of three colours, of snow, blood, and emerald. Dindrane told them the ancient story of how when Adam and Eve were turned out of paradise, Eve carried with her the bough of the tree from which she had picked the apple. She planted it, and it grew to be a tree as white as snow. Under it she lived with Adam, and it turned as green as emerald. Under it jealous Cain killed Abel, and it turned as red as blood. So it grew and flourished until the time of Solomon the Great, who built this ship and put all the marvels in it. By then the tree had white, green, and red branches, and the spindles were cut from these, and at every cut a drop of blood fell.

When Dindrane had shown them all the marvels of the ship of Solomon, it was time to gird on the sword and be going. She opened a box and took out a girdle woven in three of golden threads, set with fine stones and fastened with a magnificent buckle of gold. She told them it was woven of her hair, 'which at one time I loved well.'

She presented the sword to the knights and all agreed that Galahad should wear it. As they asked him, he consented, though he said: 'Know you well that it belongs to me no more than it does to you.' So Dindrane bound it on to Galahad and he said he was her knight all the days of his life.

They went back to their own ship, and the world of marvels was for the moment left behind. In the morning the ship drew near to the coast of Scotland, by a rock-built castle called Carteloyse. Dindrane warned them that the men of the castle were enemies of King Arthur's court, and they went on shore prepared for action. There was no surrender, and the three had to kill every man of the garrison. They found the rightful lord of the castle shut up in a dungeon and set him free. It was too late to save him, for he died almost at once, but happy in the sight of Galahad, whom he recognized as the chosen knight of God.

While they were resting a voice was heard telling them to go on to the wounded Keeper of the Hallows to cure him as soon as possible. So they set off again with Dindrane.

CHAPTER 23

THE DEATH OF DINDRANE

THE three knights and Dindrane now thought that they were drawing near their goal in the Quest of the Holy Grail. But for Dindrane it proved to be a Quest which brought her on this day not to the Holy Grail but to the Master of the Holy Grail itself, Jesus Christ.

On their way they passed a castle. A knight was on patrol outside, and at the sight of them he spurred to the highway. Instead of challenging them, he asked: 'Lords, this gentlewoman that you lead with you, is she a maiden not wed?'

Dindrane smiled and said: 'Yes, sir, I am.'

The knight leaned over and seized her bridle rein and said: 'By the Holy Cross, you shall not escape me before you have yielded to the custom of this castle.'

Sir Percivale moved his horse up. 'Let her go!' he said. 'Wherever a maiden goes, she is let go free.'

As they spoke there was a clatter of hoofs and armed men from the castle surrounded them, and with them came women carrying a big silver dish. They all declared: 'This gentlewoman must yield us the custom of this castle.'

'Why,' said Galahad, 'what is the custom of this castle?'

'Sir, any maid who passes by must fill this dish with blood from her right arm.'

All three knights instantly declared that while they lived no such attempt should be made on Dindrane. The castle knights attacked them, and a battle began which raged until dark. A truce was called. The people of the castle offered shelter in the castle for the night, under guarantee of safety and safe exit next morning. Dindrane advised them to accept, and so they all went in. The custom of the castle was then more fully explained. The lady who owned the place had been ill for a long while of an unknown malady, and an old man had said that if she could be anointed from that dish full of blood from a maiden who was a king's daughter, she would be healed.

To the alarm of the three knights, Dindrane, on hearing the story, offered to be bled. Sir Galahad tried to persuade her that if she lost so much blood she would die, but she only smiled and answered: 'Truly, if I die for her healing I shall win great worship and health of soul, and honour to my family; and one harm is better than two. So there will be no more fighting, but to-morrow I shall yield you your custom of this castle.'

Every one in the castle made great celebrations over this, and the party was lodged like royal guests. Next morning they attended the Eucharist and then Dindrane asked for the sick lady to be brought. When she arrived she was in great pain and distress, but not so great as the three companions of Dindrane. The blood-letting began, and as the dish filled Dindrane grew faint, and it was obvious her life was running out with her blood. When the dish was full she said: 'Madam, I am come to my death to heal you. Therefore, for God's love, pray for me.' Her eyes moved from one loved face to another, all weeping.

'Fair brother, Sir Percivale,' she whispered, 'I die for the healing of this lady. When I am dead, do not bury me in this country, but put me in a boat at the next haven and let me drift where chance will lead me. And as soon as you three come to the city of Sarras, to achieve the Holy Grail, you will find me arrived there. Bury me there in the spiritual place. I tell you for truth, there Sir Galahad will be buried, and you too in the same place.'

Sir Percivale nodded, weeping. As they all gazed on each other and held her hands, a voice came to them and said:

'Lords, to-morrow at the hour of prime you three must separate until events bring you to the Wounded King.'

Then a priest came and gave Dindrane the Sacrament, and so she died. On the same day the sick lady of the castle became well.

'Then Sir Percivale wrote a letter saying all that she had done for them in arduous adventures, and put it in her right hand,' says Malory. 'And so he laid her in a barge, and covered it with black silk. And so the wind arose and drove the barge from the land, and all manner of knights watched it till it was out of their sight. Then they returned all to the castle, and suddenly there fell a tempest of thunder and lightning and rain, as though all the world would have broken. It passed evensong before the tempest ceased.'

Early next day the knights left the castle and rode out into the forest. The appointed hour of prime, six o'clock in the morning, was near. With tears at parting, and prayers to be soon brought together again, they separated and each rode off alone. Where the city of Sarras was they did not know, nor how they should get there, though they had read of it as a holy city and knew that if Dindrane had spoken of it they were sure to find it.

At about the same time Sir Lancelot, also on the Quest of the Grail, lay asleep. In a vision he was told to rise and arm and enter the first ship that he found. When he awoke he saw about him a marvellous clear light, which made him cross himself, and which also entered his mind and made him happy and single-minded to obey. As he rode by the riverside in the darkness he came to a little beach, and there was the dim outline of a boat without sail or oar. He went on board, and immediately his whole being was filled with the utmost joy and sweetness and he felt that he had attained everything that he had ever wanted.

When the morning light came he found that he was in the barge where Dindrane lay.

For a month he lived in the barge, floating without sail or oar where the wind of heaven led, watching over the body of Dindrane and trusting himself in peace to God.

'If you would ask how he lived,' says Malory, 'as He that fed the people of Israel with manna in the desert, so he was fed; for every day, when he said his prayers, he was sustained with the grace of the Holy Ghost.'

One night as the barge rocked on a little beach, he heard a horse's hoofs, and a man came riding down to the water's edge. Sir Lancelot sat motionless. The man dismounted, took his saddle and bridle, and leaped into the boat.

In the darkness Sir Lancelot said: 'Sir, you are welcome.'

He heard the other draw a quick breath, and his voice came urgently: 'Sir, what is your name? For my heart inclines to you.'

'My name is Sir Lancelot du Lac.'

'Sir, then you are welcome, for you were the beginner of me in this world.'

'Ah, sir, are you Sir Galahad?' Sir Lancelot got up, knowing that his happiness was now perfect.

For six months they lived alone together in the boat with the body of Dindrane, and the time seemed to them nothing. The boat carried them to strange islands, where they had perilous adventures with beasts and wild men. At other times they drifted and watched the sky and told each other all their thoughts, and were happy in each other's company.

But this could not last for ever, and Sir Lancelot knew

that a mysterious fate was waiting for his son. One morning they came round a bend of a river and saw in a clearing of the forest a stone cross, and by it a knight all in white, on horseback and leading a white horse. Sir Lancelot knew that this strange happy time was over. The knight hailed them in God's name and said to Sir Galahad: 'Sir, you have been long enough with your father. Come out of the boat and take this horse, and go where events shall lead you in the Quest of the Holy Grail.'

Sir Galahad came to Sir Lancelot and kissed him lovingly and said: 'Fair sweet father, I do not know when I shall see you again.'

'Now, for God's sake,' said his father, 'pray that He hold me still in His service.'

So Sir Galahad went ashore and mounted the white horse, and a voice declared that they would never meet again till the Day of Judgment.

'Now, my son, Sir Galahad, since we must part and never see each other more, I pray to that high Father to keep us both.'

'Sir,' said Sir Galahad, 'no prayer avails so much as yours.'

So Sir Galahad rode into the forest. But Sir Lancelot was driven before the wind for another month, and then one midnight the boat came to rest below a rock. In the moonlight he saw a castle built on the cliffs above, and a postern gate on the rock itself. No one was to be seen, and he made his way through the winding passages and halls to the chief fortress. He found no door which was shut, but all stood open, leading from silent stair to silent room.

At last his way led to a door which was shut. He set his hand on it, but could not open it. He put out his huge strength, but the door did not even shake. Then he heard a voice from within, so piercingly sweet that he knew it came from no earthly throat, saying: 'Joy and honour be to the Father of Heaven.'

Sir Lancelot knelt down outside the door, for now he knew that the Holy Grail itself was within and he had come to the end of his Quest. But whether he would be allowed to see the holy thing or not he did not know.

'Fair sweet Father Christ!' he said, 'if ever I did anything that pleased Thee, Lord, for Thy pity have me not in anger for my sins, but show me something of that I seek.' With that the door opened, and there came out a brilliant clearness, which spread through the castle until the place was as bright as if all the torches in the world were there. Sir Lancelot rose, and would have entered, but a voice forbade him.

'Sir Lancelot, enter not!'

He knelt down on the threshold.

There was a silver table in the room, and on it the Holy Grail covered with red samite, rose red, the Grail's own colour. About it were many angels. One held a burning candle, one a cross and the ornaments of an altar. Before the Grail stood a man dressed as a priest, celebrating the Eucharist. Above the priest's hands in the air were three men, and Sir Lancelot saw two of them put the youngest looking between the priest's hands. He seemed to lift him up high and show him to the watchers. He reeled under the weight, but none of the angels moved to help him.

Seeing him about to fall, Sir Lancelot cried: 'Fair Father, Jesus Christ, take it not for sin if I help the good man,' and he rushed into the room. A fiery blast smote him back, and he fell to the ground blind, deaf, and deprived of that bodily strength which he would have used to disobey the heavenly command. Totally paralysed, he felt many hands carry him from the room as a dead man.

Next morning the inhabitants of the castle found him lying outside the shut door. They looked after him until he recovered consciousness. He asked where he was and they told him that he was in the castle of Carbonek, a place well known to him. Slowly he arose and dressed, putting on first the hair shirt he always wore next to his skin. He went to greet Pelles, the lord of the castle, and father of Elaine, the mother of Galahad. As he went Sir Lancelot turned over in his mind all that had happened since those far-off days, the strange countries he had travelled in, his long love of the Queen and his new finding of his son, and how Carbonek and the Grail had run through it all and brought him finally back to this same castle where it had all begun.

Pelles greeted him with joy. He told Sir Lancelot that Elaine was dead, which grieved him. Long they sat talking over past days, and the strange times which were come on them.

Sir Lancelot stayed four days as Pelles's guest before returning to Camelot to tell King Arthur of his Quest for the Grail. On the night before he left, as they sat in the great hall under banners and trophies, the Holy Grail filled every man's dish with the food that he most loved.

Next day he set out on the old familiar ride from Carbonek to Camelot, from the castle of the Hallows and strange spiritual happenings to the seat of daily life and government. Each time he made the journey, Carbonek had become a little more important, and now Sir Lancelot was as true a citizen of the spiritual world as he was of Camelot.

The King and Queen Guenevere were waiting for the return of the knights of the Round Table who had scattered on the Quest for the Grail. Life had gone drearily for many months in Camelot, and the news was more often of knights killed on the Quest than returned in safety. The news of the arrival of Sir Lancelot therefore was a joy scarcely believed at first. It ran through the palace from tongue to tongue, and at last the great knight knelt before the King and Queen.

As King Arthur held his friend's hand and looked in his face he saw that strange experiences had happened to him. That evening the court was dismissed and the King and Queen sat with Sir Lancelot late into the night listening to what he could tell them of his doings, of Sir Galahad, Sir Percivale, and Sir Bors, the barge and the dead maiden, and the unknown worlds where he had been.

CHAPTER 24

THE ACHIEVEMENT OF THE GRAIL

THE achievement of the Grail is a phrase used in all stories of the Holy Grail to mean two things: first the presence of any one at a celebration of the Eucharist at which the Holy Grail appeared as the cup—that person had achieved the Grail, or the goodness of life in which the Grail would so appear to him; and second, the completion of the story of the Grail, the ending of its activity on earth and its withdrawal back into heaven. This is the story of the final achievement of the Grail in both meanings, which Sir Bors told the King on his return from Sarras.

The three knights, Galahad, Bors, and Percivale, had separated, as the voice had told them, till chance should bring them together to the Wounded King. They knew that the Wounded King was Pelles, Keeper of the Hallows, wounded long ago by Sir Balin in the dolorous blow, and still unhealed. One day they all rode out of a forest from different directions and met on a cross-roads. They saluted each other, and knew that the appointed time was near. They rode together to Carbonek, and were welcomed by Pelles.

That night the Holy Grail appeared in the castle. The three knights of King Arthur were present, and three knights from Gaul, three from Ireland, and three from Denmark. On the silver table appeared the Grail and before it stood an old man on whose forehead was the name *Joseph*, and angels such as Lancelot saw, some carrying candles, one a towel, one a spear which bled into a box carried in the angel's other hand. Malory says that when the bishop was about to consecrate the bread, 'there came a figure in likeness of a child, and the visage was as red and bright as any fire, and smote himself into the bread.' Then the priest vanished and a man came out of the Holy Grail bearing the marks of the Passion of Christ, who said to them: 'My knights and servants, and my true children who have come out of fleshly life into the spiritual life, I will no longer conceal myself from you, but you shall see now a part of my secrets and of my hidden things.'

Then He gave the Sacrament to all the knights, and spoke again to Galahad.

'Now you have seen that which you most desired to see. But yet you have not seen it as openly as you shall see it in the city of Sarras, in the spiritual place. Therefore you must go hence and bear with you this holy vessel, for this night it shall depart from the realm of Britain and it shall never more be seen here. And know you why? Because it is not served or worshipped as is right by those of this land, for they are turned to evil living, and therefore I shall disinherit them of the honour which I have done them. Therefore go you three to-morrow to the sea, where you will find your ship ready. Also take with you of the blood of this spear to anoint the Wounded King, and he shall have his health. And two of you will die in my service and one of you will come again and tell tidings.' Then He blessed them all and vanished.

The knights obeyed exactly. First Sir Galahad dipped his finger in the blood of the holy spear and anointed Pelles, whose wound was instantly healed. So the injury done by the dolorous blow of Sir Balin was cured. Then they rode down to the river and found a ship ready for the sea. They did not know where they were to go, for they did not know where the 'city of Sarras' was. They had often heard of it, for it was spoken of in stories, but they knew no one who had found it and come back. Sarras was a city called the 'spiritual place,' which meant two things: a place outside the realm of Britain where the Hallows had their home in the world, which many people knew of but which was only reached by a few, after long searching; and also a state of happiness and goodness in the nature of man outside his everyday state, open to any one to attain, but in this life only known now and then and not as an everyday condition.

When the three knights went on board the ship they found the silver table and the Holy Grail covered with red samite. A long while they knelt before it. When they rose it seemed they had been at sea for days, and they slept, and when they awoke they saw before them the city of Sarras.

As the ship drew in beside the quay they saw the barge wherein Sir Percivale had laid the body of his sister Dindrane. 'Truly,' said Sir Percivale, 'well has my sister kept her bond.' Then they took out of their ship the table of silver and carried it ashore.

At the gate of the city a cripple man whom they asked to help them was healed and carried the table as nimbly as Sir Galahad. When the Grail was safely housed they went down to the harbour again and brought up the body of Dindrane and buried her as richly as became a king's daughter.

The lord of the castle soon heard that they had brought the Grail. He was afraid that his power would come to an end, and so he seized the three knights and imprisoned them in a deep hole. Little had they expected this on such a mission, but there was no escape. They were sustained by the Holy Grail, which came to them constantly and brought to each of them the food he most desired, and complete happiness of mind. So they lived for a year, and then the lord fell ill and sent for the knights and set them free. He died, and while the city council was dismayed by the problem of who should succeed him a voice sounded among them telling them to choose the youngest of the three knights, who was Sir Galahad.

So Sir Galahad became King of Sarras. By his instructions the silver table was enclosed in a chest of gold and precious stones, and every day early in the morning the three knights came before it and said their prayers.

On the first anniversary of the day Sir Galahad became king, the knights as usual went early to their prayers, but this time they found the Holy Grail out of the chest and a man kneeling before it in the appearance of a bishop, surrounded by a great fellowship of angels. The knights knelt, and the bishop began to celebrate the Eucharist. When he had consecrated, he turned to the knights and called Sir Galahad to him, saying: 'Come forth, servant of Jesus Christ, and you will see that which you have much desired to see.'

Then Sir Galahad began to tremble as in the mortal flesh he began to approach spiritual things. 'Lord, I thank Thee,' he said, 'for now I see that which has been my desire many a day.'

Therewith the bishop gave him the Sacrament.

Then Sir Galahad went to Sir Percivale and kissed him and commended him to God. Next he went to Sir Bors and kissed him and commended him to God and said: 'My fair lord, salute me unto my lord Sir Lancelot my father, and bid him remember this unstable world.'

He turned away and knelt down before the table, and suddenly his soul departed and a crowd of angels carried it up to heaven in the sight of his two friends. Then they saw a hand come down from heaven, and take the Holy

Grail and the spear, and carry them up to heaven. Since then no man can say that he has seen the Holy Grail.

When the Hallows were withdrawn there ended also the chance to establish in Britain a truly good state, in which all men could serve both God and the King and be both good and happy. The attempt of King Arthur to make Britain as like heaven as possible, through his knights of the Round Table, was now bound to fail. Because men had not turned to good living at the appearance of the Hallows, but had tried, like Sir Balin, to use them for personal pride or for safety, the Hallows had produced quarrelling and bloodshed instead of peace and love. So they withdrew back into heaven at this 'achievement' or 'completion' of the Grail, and the great attempt of King Arthur began to break down.

When the two knights realized that Sir Galahad was dead they were tempted to fall into despair. But they remembered their faith, and held together. They buried him by Dindrane in holy ground within the city, and immediately afterwards Sir Percivale retired into a hermitage outside in the country and became a monk. Sir Bors was constantly with him but did not become a monk, for he meant some day to go back to Britain. Sir Percivale lived a year and two months in the hermitage and then died. Sir Bors buried him beside Sir Galahad and Dindrane.

Thus Sir Bors was left alone, in a world that knew nothing of him or his friends, of their lives and struggles and adventures. He put on his armour again and came down to the harbour, and went on board a ship. 'By good adventure he came unto the realm of Britain, and so he rode apace till he came to Camelot where the King was.'

He had been gone so long that they had given him up for dead. He looked round on the faces he had known since he had come to the court as a young nephew of Sir

Lancelot, and he saw that they were all old men. In the grand effort of King Arthur after justice and good life some had grown old in a good way and some in a careless way, but a lifetime had passed and the end had come. He stood a moment with his hand over his eyes. The King made a sign and dismissed the court except for Sir Lancelot and the secretaries. They wrote down the reports of the knights who came back from the Quest of the Grail, to be made into books which were kept in the library in Salisbury.

Night fell on Sir Bors's tale, and the logs burned low on the hearth, forgotten as the King and Queen and Sir Lancelot sat motionless, listening. The King knew that with the withdrawal of the Grail lesser days had come on Britain, and the hope of a strange, happy goodness was gone. He was middle-aged, his Round Table was broken, and the glory of the Grail was gone.

At last they moved. The King dismissed the secretaries, and retired with the Queen. Sir Bors and Sir Lancelot were left alone. Then Sir Bors told him the last words of Sir Galahad. A gleam passed over Sir Lancelot's dark face.

'Now I trust to God,' he said, 'his prayer will help me.' He laid his arm across his nephew's shoulders and looked down at him from his great height.

'You are very welcome! All that I may ever do for you or yours, you will find my poor body ready to do while breath is in it. That I promise you faithfully, never to fail. And know well, gentle nephew Sir Bors, you and I will never part while our lives last.'

'Sir,' said Sir Bors, 'as you will, so will I.'

4

THE END OF THE ROUND TABLE

CHAPTER 25

SIR LANCELOT AND THE LILY MAID OF ASTOLAT

THE Round Table was scattered on the Quest of the Holy Grail. A few knights had returned but the court was empty and spiritless. It was hot summer weather, and King Arthur decided to hold a tournament to keep up their spirits and their practice in arms.

Sometimes Sir Lancelot did not fight in these jousts because he always won and it discouraged the young and more feeble spirited and gave rise to tricks and foul play by the more unpleasant. On this occasion he thought he would fight in disguise on the other side, in one of the visiting teams. It was always possible to join a team on the day of the joust, and a knight could keep on his helmet and not show his face. If he had a good horse and armour and knew the rules of chivalry he was welcome.

The tournament was to be in Camelot, or Winchester as we know it. The court was in London, so they all rode down through the leafy lanes and harvest fields of Surrey and Hampshire. On the way they lodged at Astolat, which was probably Guildford. Behind them, in new armour, visor down, rode Sir Lancelot, his shield with the famous gold leopards on a blue ground hidden under a covering.

Astolat was full and busy with the arrival of the court. But it had a castle in which lived an old-fashioned family who did not mix much with the great world. The lady of the castle was dead, and old Sir Bernard had brought up his two sons and one daughter in a quiet simple way. The sons, Torre and Lavaine, were newly made knights, and the daughter Elaine was her father's darling, young, beautiful, and good, and dearly loved by all the people, who called her the Lily Maid of Astolat.

The old quiet castle did not attract the people of the court, but Lancelot rode there and was given courteous welcome, though no one knew him. When they had all made friends, Lancelot explained that he wanted to joust unrecognized, which was quite usual, and asked if he might borrow a plain shield, and leave his there to pick up on his way back. Sir Bernard said that his eldest son, Sir Torre, had been hurt in his first joust and could not go to the tournament, and that the visitor could have his shield. He asked him to take with him Lavaine, his younger son, whose first joust it would be.

The men stood talking, and Elaine listened silently, too shy at first to look much at the stranger or to speak, but

Won by the mellow voice before she look'd.

Gradually she began to look up at him, and saw the tall, strong figure, the dark hair and scarred sunburnt face, the deep eyes that looked on all men with love, but with one love only on the Queen.

He seemed the goodliest man
That ever among ladies ate in hall,
And noblest, when she lifted up her eyes.
However marr'd, of more than twice her years,
Seam'd with an ancient swordcut on the cheek,
And bruised and bronzed, she lifted up her eyes
And loved him, with that love which was her doom.

The evening passed, and Sir Lancelot told the family tales of the King's wars and his two aims—to break the heathen by fighting and to beat down the evil in man by knightly vows and life.

Early next morning he and Lavaine got ready to go. Elaine came to them, and asked very shyly if Sir Lancelot would wear her favour at the tournament. He answered that he had never done that in his life, not saying that the reason was that he was the true knight only of the Queen. Elaine replied that that would make it all the more complete a disguise for him, and moved by this idea Sir Lancelot accepted. He tied the favour, a red sleeve sewn with pearls, on his helmet. Sir Lavaine brought him his brother's shield and Lancelot asked Elaine to keep his shield for him till he came again. Then the knights rode away, followed by their squires.

On the way to Camelot, Sir Lancelot told Lavaine who he was. The young man gave his promise to keep the secret. Meanwhile Elaine at home had taken the stranger's shield up to her room and had started to make a cover for it, copying the design of the gold leopards on blue in embroidery.

The tournament day arrived, and Sir Lancelot and Sir Lavaine rode out to Camelot quietly and came round by a lane to a little leafy wood bordering on the ground of the teams opposing the King. Sir Lancelot was wearing the red sleeve on his helmet. They waited in hiding while the teams lined up, the trumpets blew, and the opening charges were made. Against King Arthur were the lords of North Wales and of Northumberland and many others. Sir Lancelot's expert eye followed every move. Lavaine, his lance ready, waited quivering for the word of command. One knight after another on each side charged and the battle began to take shape. King Arthur's side pressed the others hard.

'See that group of good knights,' said Sir Lancelot

through his visor, 'they hold together like boars chased by hounds. Now, with your help, we shall make those knights who are chasing these fellows on our side go back as fast as they are now coming forward.'

He fixed his eye on the nerve centre of the fight and charged right in. His first impact sent flying five knights: Sir Kay, Sir Brandiles, Sir Sagramour, Sir Dodinas, and Sir Griflet. Young Lavaine sent down two good knights: Sir Lucan and Sir Bedivere. Lancelot did not pause. That was part of the secret of his superiority in fighting. He gave no one time to recover or to think. Before half the side knew that he had joined in, he had unhorsed seven more, and Lavaine another. But in the next charge, Sir Lancelot's horse was hurled to the ground, and Sir Bors's spear pierced Sir Lancelot's side and broke off.

When Lavaine saw the horse fall, he wheeled to the King of the Scots, who happened to be unguarded, and knocked him off his horse. He seized the bridle and forced his way right in and held every one off while Sir Lancelot got on to the horse. Then began a fight that no one ever forgot. Sir Lancelot thought that he must die of his wound, and he was determined to die well. Nobody could match him. He struck down Sir Bors, Sir Ector, Sir Lionel, and three more. The first three got on horseback again and charged him. He sent them flying again, and performed the final act of victory on each by taking off their helmets and proving that if he wished he could cut off their heads. A knight so defeated was out of the battle. Forty knights did these two champions strike down, Sir Lancelot thirty and Sir Lavaine ten. The match was won, and the King and the Round Table had lost.

The King gave the sign and the trumpets blew to lodging. The heralds announced that the prize was awarded to the knight wearing the red sleeve. But the knight was nowhere to be found. At the trumpet's sound he had turned and ridden fast into the leafy wood, followed by Sir Lavaine, feeling his wound grow on him as the heat of battle died away.

An old friend of his, once knight and now hermit and doctor, lived in the woods, and Sir Lancelot rode there fast. He was almost unconscious when they arrived. The hermit recognized him at once. He carried him in with Sir Lavaine, and began a fight to save his life.

Meantime King Arthur ordered a search to be made for the victor knight. Sir Gawaine organized a hunt round Camelot but without success. So the prize was not awarded, and the court returned to London. On the way back Sir Gawaine happened to lodge at the castle in Astolat. The family received him eagerly and pressed him for news of the tournament. When Sir Gawaine heard their story, and discovered that the knight with the red sleeve had left his shield in the castle he begged to see it. As soon as he saw the gold leopards on the blue ground, he cried out: 'Sir Lancelot!'

So the news was told, and Sir Bors, who had wounded him, was stricken to the heart, for he loved Sir Lancelot more than any one in the world. Elaine, the Lily Maid, persuaded her father to let her ride out in search of the wounded knight and Sir Lavaine. By luck she came on her brother exercising his horse in a field, and told him of Sir Gawaine's coming and persuaded him to lead her to Sir Lancelot. From then on she never left the wounded man but nursed him day and night.

Days passed, and he lay desperately ill. Then came Sir Bors, who had found him at last, and stood beside the bed in such grief as made Sir Lancelot's eyes twinkle, and he said: 'Cheer up, cousin, all is welcome that God sends. If I had not been so full of pride I would have said who I was and you would not have wounded me. Let us say no more about it, but talk of something else and find a remedy to make me well quickly.'

Gradually the battle for his life was won, and at last he lay out of danger, and convalescent. Slowly he grew better, and was able to sit on his horse and do more each day. At last came the day which Elaine was dreading, when they left the hermitage and went back into the world, to the castle at Astolat. Eventually he was well enough to leave Astolat and return to court.

Elaine knew that she could not go back to her former life without him. She asked her father and her two brothers to come with her, and went to Sir Lancelot.

'My lord, Sir Lancelot,' she said, 'now I see you are really going away. Fair and courteous knight, have mercy on me, and do not let me die for your love.'

Sir Lancelot had never run away from difficulties in his life. He did not now.

'What do you want me to do?' he asked gravely.

'Sir, marry me,' she said.

'My dear, thank you from my heart, but I am resolved never to be a married man.'

'Then I shall die for love of you.'

'You will not,' answered Sir Lancelot. 'I am twice your age, my dear, and you will grow to love me differently. You will not always feel like this. Some day you will meet a young man your own age, and all my life you may call on me to fight for you and be your knight.'

'Sir, of all this I will have nothing. But if you will not marry me, I warn you, Sir Lancelot, my good days are done.'

But Sir Lancelot answered: 'That I cannot do.'

Elaine gave a cry and fell unconscious on the ground. Her women carried her away to her room. There was silence. Sir Lancelot picked up his belt and gloves and was ready to go. Turning to young Lavaine he asked him harshly if he was still willing to follow him.

'Sir, how can I help following you unless you order me to leave you?'

So Sir Lancelot and Lavaine rode away.

Elaine lay motionless on her bed. For nine days and nights she lay without eating, drinking, or sleeping, and uttering no sound but Sir Lancelot's name. Every day the people gathered at the castle gate and wept at the news of the fading of their Lily Maid.

On the tenth day she roused herself. She spoke of her love and said she did no wrong because all kinds of love come from God. She asked her father to write her short history in a letter and put the letter in her hand as soon as she was dead, to dress her in her finest clothes and lay her in a barge draped all in black, to put their old dumb man-servant in charge and let the river carry her to London to the King's palace at Westminster. There the court and Sir Lancelot would see her and read the letter and give her burial.

King Arthur and Queen Guenevere were sitting talking in a deep window seat overlooking the river. Into their view glided the black-draped barge, with one white figure lying in it and one old oarsman sitting at the helm. It was guided to the palace steps and there remained, rocking gently, while neither traveller made a sign. The King and Queen went hand in hand to look on the Lily Maid who lay there. Slowly the knights gathered round, and then came Sir Lancelot. The King took the letter from her hand and read it. Elaine's last message was:

'Most noble knight, my lord Sir Lancelot, now has death separated us two for love of you. I loved you, and I was called the Lily Maid of Astolat. Therefore unto all ladies I tell my sad story, but do you pray for my soul and give me burial. This is my last request. Pray for my soul, Sir Lancelot, as you are peerless.'

All eyes were on Sir Lancelot as the letter ended. He told the King that Elaine's death had not been his fault, and called Sir Lavaine, her brother, to prove it. 'She was both fair and good, and I owed much to her, but she loved me beyond measure.'

When the whole story was told, the Lily Maid was carried into the palace. Next day the court attended her burial, which was performed as magnificently as for a queen. Then the dumb man rowed the barge home to the mourning castle of Astolat.

CHAPTER 26

THE QUEEN AND THE POISONED APPLE

AFTER the Quest of the Holy Grail had been concluded, and all those knights who had survived had come back to court, there was a feeling of anticlimax. The knights of the Round Table had waited twenty years for the coming of the knight who was to fill the Siege Perilous, and had worked hard fighting the heathen and restoring safety and peace to Britain. Now Sir Galahad had sat in the siege and had brought to an earthly end the adventures of the Holy Grail and had died in the completion of them, so that all that interest was over; a new generation of heathen was beginning to invade the coast; many of the knights were middle-aged and the fighting had all to be done again without the enthusiasm of newness and the marvels of the Holy Grail.

The knights were in low spirits, and idle quarrels became too important. Sir Lancelot took every opportunity to keep away from court and go on patrols and fighting expeditions. One day when he was away the Queen gave a dinner, and asked twenty-four of the senior knights. Among them was Sir Gawaine, who was known to have an appetite for fruit, especially apples and pears. Any host took special care over them when Sir Gawaine was coming to dinner. The Queen also asked Gawaine's brothers, Agravaine, Gaheris, and Gareth, and his half-brother Mordred. These with Gawaine made up the Orkney clan, who had all conspired to murder Sir Lamorak years ago. Among the other guests was Sir Pinel, who was cousin to

Sir Lamorak but who never said anything about it and bided his time for vengeance. With these came Sir Bors and Sir Kay, Sir Palomides, and all the well-known figures.

If Sir Lancelot had been there nothing disgraceful would have happened. But Sir Pinel saw his chance. He poisoned some apples and arranged them in the dish nearest to Sir Gawaine. Dinner went on, there was music, the Queen was gay; they talked of Sir Lancelot, and wondered with what great feat of arms he would reappear. The time came for dessert. Sir Pinel watched Sir Gawaine between the candles. But poison was a clumsy choice of weapon. Sir Gawaine was talking, and Sir Patrise, next to him, took an apple and ate it. When Sir Patrise had eaten it, he swelled until he burst, and fell down dead among them all.

Uproar broke out. Sir Pinel kept his head and said nothing. Every one naturally suspected the Queen, who had arranged the dinner. Sir Gawaine was convinced that the poison had been meant for him because an apple had been chosen. Sir Bors tried to make him be quiet, but his wild Orkney nature could not be controlled, and he stood up frantically and accused the Queen. Guenevere stood like a statue, silent, seeing it was a plot, and thinking it was aimed at her because Sir Lancelot was not there to defend her. As she did not answer, and no one spoke up for her defence, Sir Mador de la Porte, cousin to Sir Patrise, plucked up courage as he seemed to be on the winning side, challenged the Queen and accused her of the murder of his cousin.

After that there could be no drawing back. The King was fetched, the charge repeated, and the penalty of death by burning was demanded. The method of trial was a battle between the accuser and a champion of the accused. The decision was thus in God's hands. The King realized that he was forbidden by his own laws from fighting for his wife, but felt sure that a champion would come forward, so he told Sir Mador to ask for a day for trial. Sir Mador then pointed out that none of the knights at the dinner would fight for the Queen, as they all believed her guilty. This disposed of all the good fighters of the court, and the King knew at once that it was a deadly blow. Sir Mador saw the King's face change, and he immediately made the formal request for a day for the trial. The King chose the longest space of time that the law allowed, and fixed a day fifteen days from then. Sir Mador was to appear armed in the meadow outside Camelot. If a champion appeared for the Queen, God would reveal the right; if none appeared, then the Queen must be burned; she would be at the stake before the contest, ready for the judgment. 'I am answered,' said Sir Mador, and the King dismissed them all.

Then the King and Queen alone together had a desperate discussion: how to find Sir Lancelot, and what to do if he could not be found.

'What is the matter with you?' said the King, 'that you cannot keep Sir Lancelot on your side?' Then he thought of Sir Lancelot's closest friend, Sir Bors. True he had been at the dinner, but he might defend the Queen for Sir Lancelot's sake. The Queen went that night to Sir Bors's apartments and made her request.

He was most embarrassed by it. He had joined with the other knights in suspecting her, and they would think he was deliberately defending the guilty just because she was the Queen. But when the King added his request to the Queen's, then Sir Bors promised to fight as her champion unless a better knight than he should come forward. The Queen wept with relief, and the King could say nothing, but took his hand and pressed it silently.

Next day Sir Bors had news that Sir Lancelot was on his

way back. He promptly left the court, without taking his squire, or telling any one where he was going, and rode to meet him. He told him the whole story, and Sir Lancelot felt sure that it was a plot against the Queen. He immediately laid his plans and considered the weaknesses of Sir Mador as his enemy. Sir Lancelot, like all good generals, never underestimated his enemy, and left nothing to chance.

'This has worked out just as I might have chosen,' he said to Sir Bors. 'Now you get ready for the fight, right up to the last moment, and try to delay things as much as you can, because you know Sir Mador gets much too excited when there is any action, and the longer he is kept waiting the wilder he will be when the battle begins.'

'Sir, let me handle him,' said Sir Bors.

So Sir Bors went back to court that evening, and announced that he was going to fight for the Queen. Many of the knights objected, as he had known they would. He answered them: 'Lords, it seems to me you speak as you should not, for she has always been a maintainer of good knights, and the most generous lady with her gifts and her friendliness that I ever saw or heard of. It would be a shame to all of us if we allowed her to be burned without striking a blow for her. So I tell you all that I will not allow it, for I do not think the Queen is guilty of Sir Patrise's death. She had no quarrel with him, nor with any of us twenty-four who were at dinner, and I am sure that it will be proved later, whatever it looks like now, that there was treason among us.'

Some of the knights came over to his side and agreed with him, and some did not. So the time went on, and the fifteenth morning came, and every one crowded to the jousting meadow. Instead of the usual gay mass of tents for all contesting knights, and the decorations, flags, and stalls, the space was bare except for one tent at each end, and opposite the royal stand a grim enclosure with a huge pile made ready to burn round an iron stake. In this enclosure, guarded by the Constable of Britain, sat the Queen. In the royal stand sat King Arthur alone.

Everywhere else the ground was black with people. Never had such a crowd been seen before. Punctually on time a herald blew and Sir Mador rode on to the ground, saluted the King, and in a voice echoing hollowly through his visor made his accusation against the Queen. The answering herald blew, and on rode Sir Bors, saluted the King, and declared the accusation false. Sir Mador, who was very wrought up, demanded to join battle at once. Sir Bors delayed with some of the formal appeals and declarations which were permissible in such an encounter, and held matters up for some time. Finally they retired to their tents and took their arms and prepared. Out rode Sir Mador, lance couched, his horse's neck lathered with excitement caught from his rider. He cantered round the field shouting his challenge: 'Bid your champion come forth if he dare.'

Hidden in the wood, Sir Lancelot watched him, noting every detail of his seat, his lance grip, the slant of his shield. He was circling a second time, the crowd were whispering, the King was glancing uneasily at Sir Bors's tent, when out from the wood there rode a stranger knight bearing an unknown shield, riding a white horse at full gallop. Sir Bors rode out to meet him; there was a parley; the stranger claimed the right to be the Queen's champion. The new knight was big and grim, and rode, one would say, almost as well as Sir Lancelot. Challenges were exchanged, the King agreed, Sir Bors withdrew, and Sir Mador faced the strange knight down the length of the list.

The first charge brought Sir Mador down, and the

Queen's heart leaped, for in that riding and that stroke she had recognized Sir Lancelot. They fought on foot, and Sir Mador strove desperately against the grim figure that stalked after him and smote blow on blow. But at last Sir Lancelot struck him down, and stood over him unlacing his helmet to cut off his head. Sir Mador prayed for his life, and acquitted the Queen of his accusation.

'I will only grant you your life on condition that you never raise this accusation again, and that no mention is made on Sir Patrise's tomb of the Queen's name.'

Then Sir Mador withdrew with his supporters to his tent. The strange knight walked across to the stairs of the royal stand. By that time the Queen had been released and had joined the King. They both came down the stairs and greeted and thanked the knight, and took him back into the stand for a glass of wine. As he took off his helmet there was a general shout of 'Lancelot!' and 'Du Lac!' The King took both his hands, the Queen burst into tears, and round them gathered Sir Lancelot's family and all his friends, full of questions, exclamations, and joy.

So it all ended happily, though it had at one time looked otherwise for the Queen. The mystery of who had poisoned the apple was not unravelled until an enchantress, named Nimue, came to court. She declared the guilty knight was Sir Pinel, and he proved the story by fleeing from court and going into hiding abroad. Then Sir Mador tried to be restored in the Queen's favour and after a suitable time Sir Lancelot interceded for him with the Queen, and all was forgiven.

CHAPTER 27

SIR MELIAGRAUNCE

ALTHOUGH Sir Lancelot had rescued the Queen in the affair of the poisoned apple, the attempt to dishonour her had been made, and might be made again. The Queen was beautiful, and there were plenty of bad or reckless knights who would not hesitate to take a chance to kidnap her, always providing that Sir Lancelot was elsewhere at the time.

Sir Meliagraunce, who was a coward and a thoroughly unworthy man, had thought himself in love with the Queen for a long time. His love was of the kidnapping and not the knightly kind, and he waited for a chance when Sir Lancelot was away. It came on May Day. The court was this year in London. The Queen had arranged a party early on May morning, to ride out into the woods and fields opposite Westminster to bring home the may. Sir Lancelot was at a council with the King and could not come, so the Queen went out without him. She was accompanied by ten knights and ten ladies, and each knight had a squire and two servants. All were unarmed, wearing green silk for May Day and carrying only light court swords.

Sir Meliagraunce lived in a castle seven miles from Westminster, and there he had large troops of men-at-arms and archers. 'So, when the Queen was out on her maying with all her knights who were bedecked with leaves, mosses, and flowers in the freshest manner, there came out of the wood Sir Meliagraunce with eightscore men, all prepared for fighting and taking prisoners, and ordered the Queen and her knights to halt.'

'Traitor knight,' said the Queen, 'what are you thinking of? Will you bring shame on yourself? Remember you are a knight of the Round Table; pause before you dishonour the noble King who made you knight. You shame all knighthood and yourself and me.'

'As for all this fine talk,' replied Sir Meliagraunce, 'that is all very well. Understand, madam, that I have loved you many a year, and never till now could I get you at such a disadvantage. And therefore I will take you as I find you.'

At this discourteous speech the Queen's knights fell on Sir Meliagraunce and his men, without armour and with no hope of success. They laid about them with such skill that they killed forty of the enemy before they themselves were all disabled. When the Queen saw that they were wounded and surrounded, she cried to Sir Meliagraunce that she would yield to him on condition that her knights were spared and were brought with her and lodged wherever she was lodged. Sir Meliagraunce gave way, though he had meant to kill them all and take only the Queen, but time was passing and he was afraid some hidden watcher in the woods might send a message to Sir Lancelot. He meant to be safe inside his castle wall before that happened.

It was the Queen who outwitted him. While the wounded men were being helped on to horses and every one was preparing to set out to the castle, the Queen had a word with a young page, a boy of twelve, who rode a fast fresh pony.

'When you see a chance,' she said, 'slip away and take this ring to Sir Lancelot du Lac, and pray him as he loves me to rescue me. And don't spare your horse. Don't slacken for water or for land.'

The boy was on fire with pride and determination, and took the first chance that offered, when the big horses were crowding across a little stream and he had to wait until they were over. He turned his pony and spurred down a hedge path, and though some of Meliagraunce's men chased him he got away.

Sir Meliagraunce knew what that meant. Sir Lancelot would arrive. He hurried the Queen and the knights into the castle, and sent thirty archers to ambush Sir Lancelot, telling them to shoot especially at his horse, for he had no faith that even thirty of them could overcome the great knight himself. The Queen insisted on having the ten wounded knights in her apartments, where she and her ladies looked after them and nursed them. Shut out, Sir Meliagraunce cursed and paced about the castle, preparing for a state of siege against the inevitable arrival of the Queen's champion.

The page made his way safely out of the woods and galloped his pony at full speed along the open road to Westminster. The Queen's ring won him instant admission to the city and palace and Sir Lancelot's apartments. The great knight was just returning with his retinue from the King's council. At the words, 'A page with the Queen's ring,' he halted and summoned the boy. He looked closely at the ring and as he heard the story his colour changed and one of his rare angers came over him. There was no more talking then. His armour was brought, his horse prepared, and a message sent to Sir Lavaine to follow him, and within the hour he was going as hard as the heavy charger would carry him down the road to the woods. It had not occurred to him to take a troop of men-at-arms or knights with him; he meant to settle this alone.

Coming down to the river at Westminster he met a group of pack-horses and drivers taking all the road over the bridge, so he rode his horse straight down the bank into the water and swam, armed as he was, across to Lambeth. From there he made straight for the place where he knew the Queen had gone maying. The trampled earth showed the battle-ground, and soon he was riding hard on the tracks of the company going back to the castle. Suddenly the men in ambush sprang out on him and shot his horse. Raging, Sir Lancelot came at them on foot with his huge sword. They all turned and ran.

Sir Lancelot tramped on, over ditches and through wet fields in his heavy armour, getting more and more angry. He heard the welcome sound of a horse, and a woodman's cart came down the path with two carters in it. It was one of the rules of etiquette that no knight could ride in a cart. Sir Lancelot was too much in earnest to care. He asked the carters if they would drive him to the castle, two miles off. The driver refused. Sir Lancelot scrambled into the cart and gave the man such a blow with his mailed fist that he fell over backwards, dead. The other carter hastily said that he would drive the knight wherever he wanted, and so Sir Lancelot came to the castle.

The Queen and her ladies were sitting restlessly in a bay window, refusing all converse with Sir Meliagraunce and his men, watching and waiting for Sir Lancelot. Up the winding approach from the woods to the castle gates came a horse and cart, and as they watched it idly the Queen gave a cry, for she saw standing up in the cart an armed knight. She sprang up, and her ladies pressed to the window. 'Now I shall prove how lucky is that person who has a trusty friend!' she cried. 'Aha! I see well you were hard put to it when you had to ride in that cart.'

Sir Lancelot arrived, unhorsed and alone, at the castle gate. Lifting his visor, he roared in a voice which rang over the wall and in at all the arrow slits and windows:

Sir Lancelot held the whole castle at bay

'Where are you, false traitor Sir Meliagraunce, knight of the Round Table? Come out, you traitor, you and all your gang, for I am here, Sir Lancelot du Lac, to fight with you all.' He seized the little gate and hurled it back on the porter who was hurrying down to lock it, and smote the man under the ear so that he broke his neck and killed him. He stepped into the archway and then into the courtyard and every one hid from him and kept dead quiet. He held the whole castle at bay.

Sir Meliagraunce was terrified. He ran to the Queen while Sir Lancelot raged in the courtyard, and yielded himself to her mercy, imploring her to save him from Sir Lancelot. The Queen went swiftly down the winding stairs and out into the courtyard and took Sir Lancelot by both hands. He was still shouting for the traitor knight to come out and face him. The Queen laughed gently at him, and thanked him for his coming and said: 'The knight is sorely regretting this whole misadventure that he has embarked on.'

Sir Lancelot, still half angry about his dead horse, answered gruffly: 'Madam, if I had known you had made it up with him so easily I wouldn't have made such haste to get to you.'

The Queen held his arm and smiled at him. 'Why do you say that? Are you sorry you have done so well? You know I never made it up with him because I liked him, but to stop a brawl and scandal.'

'Madam, you know I would never like slander and talk. But no one except my lord King Arthur and you, madam, could stop me from killing Sir Meliagraunce before I go away.'

'I know that well,' she answered gently. 'You shall have everything arranged as you decide.'

Sir Lancelot's wrath died, and he smiled back at her.

'Madam, so long as you are pleased, it pleases me,' and they went upstairs together to confront Sir Meliagraunce.

Trial by battle was arranged, eight days from then, in the fields beside Westminster. Sir Meliagraunce withdrew, heavy-hearted, bent on getting out of it by one means or another. Sir Lancelot went to talk to the ten wounded knights, and after that every one settled down to spend the day resting and looking after the sick men. The next day they would all return to Westminster.

Sir Meliagraunce invited Sir Lancelot to inspect the castle. He had made some arrangements beforehand, and on the tour Sir Lancelot trod on an unfastened trap-door and fell into a deep cellar on to a pile of straw. Sir Meliagraunce fastened the trap-door and went back to his rooms. When inquiry was made he professed to know nothing of the visitor's whereabouts, and every one thought that Sir Lancelot had suddenly left the castle and gone back to Westminster. He often made these unexpected departures and arrivals, which were a safeguard in times of danger.

Meantime Sir Lavaine arrived, and next morning escorted the Queen and her party back to court. When they arrived the Queen was surprised not to find Sir Lancelot, but every one assumed he was on some business of his own.

But next day Sir Meliagraunce appeared, not looking at all like a man who was due to fight Sir Lancelot in a week. He was almost airy about his behaviour to the Queen and swaggered about in a way which amazed every one. He kept this up day after day, until the Queen became uneasy. She spoke to several knights, and every one agreed that Sir Meliagraunce's behaviour combined with Sir Lancelot's absence looked as if some mischief had been worked. Sir Lavaine asked for the privilege of fighting instead of the champion, if by any evil chance it should be necessary. The King granted it, saying he was sure some treachery had been done.

All this time Sir Lancelot was shut up in the dark dungeon without sight of day. Food and drink were brought to him by the wife of one of the castle officers, who tried, like all women who came in contact with Sir Lancelot, to make him unfaithful to his vow to the Queen. She offered to set him free if he would become her knight. Politely but persistently Sir Lancelot refused. He knew his vow represented the ideal of honour and knighthood, on which the importance of the Queen was based, and it was more important to keep that and trust to God than to think there was no help but in his own strong arm and be ready to break his vow to use that arm.

Early in the morning of the battle day the lady's heart gave way. She knew that if she kept Sir Lancelot prisoner he would hate her for ever, and if she let him free in time he would at least remember her with goodwill for that.

So Sir Lancelot escaped, in the nick of time. The heralds were sounding and Sir Lavaine was ready at his end of the ground when there was a commotion in the crowd and the great horse and rider came thundering on to the field. Roars went up as he was recognized. Saluting the King, he told every one in a loud voice how Sir Meliagraunce had trapped him. The cheering changed to howls and hisses, and the crowd prepared for another of Sir Lancelot's victories.

But Sir Meliagraunce was a trickster to the last. The heralds blew, the knights withdrew to their ends of the lists, lances were poised, the trumpet sounded, and they charged. Sir Meliagraunce came off his horse, and Sir Lancelot dismounted and approached sword in hand. But Sir Meliagraunce refused to fight. He yielded himself in the most grovelling language that chivalry allowed, and

Early in the morning of the battle day the lady's heart gave way

called on Sir Lancelot as a fellow knight of the Round Table not to kill him. He had forfeited all the privileges of knighthood by disregarding its responsibilities and using violence to the Queen and treachery to Sir Lancelot, and yet he claimed them now to save himself. Sir Lancelot hesitated. He could not bring himself to kill a man who grovelled on the ground and would not get up and fight, but if he let him go he knew he would be treacherous again.

'Get up, man,' he exclaimed, 'and fight!'

'Not I,' replied Sir Meliagraunce, who was trading on Sir Lancelot's chivalry and knew he was safe while he refused to fight. 'I will never get up until you agree that I have yielded.'

'Well, I will make you an offer,' said Sir Lancelot. 'I will take my helmet off, and all the armour down my left side, and I will have my left arm tied behind me, and I will fight you like that.'

Sir Meliagraunce started up. Such a handicap had never been heard of.

'My lord Arthur,' he shouted, 'you heard this offer; remember it, because I am going to accept it. Have him disarmed and bound according to his own offer.'

The King spoke uneasily to his friend: 'You cannot mean that, Sir Lancelot; you spoke in heat, you cannot keep such terms.'

'I will, my lord, for I will never go back on my word.'

Every one's heart sank as the disarming began. Protests arose all round the field, and the King and Queen fell silent. Only the enemies of the King, Sir Mordred and Sir Agravaine, and the evil men who plotted with them, leaned forward and suddenly drew breath. If Lancelot were killed, who knew what chance for evil might open in the kingdom?

Sir Lancelot was ready, his head, neck, half his body, and

his left leg bare, and his arm tied behind him. Most men could not even lift their swords with one hand only, still less use them. Sir Lancelot knew that the odds against him were so heavy that the first encounter could settle it. He was not afraid. He thought of the King, and that here was a traitor to the King's order of knighthood, and such it had always been his duty to kill. Sir Meliagraunce rushed in. There was a flash as Sir Lancelot sprang aside and forward. Sir Meliagraunce missed, Sir Lancelot's sword swung as he leaped, and there was a crash. Sir Lancelot stood waiting to be unbound, and men dragged Sir Meliagraunce off the field by his legs. His head and helmet were split in two.

Roar upon roar went up from the crowd. Men rushed to release Sir Lancelot and bring him a cloak and lead him to the King. Sir Mordred and Sir Agravaine sat back and waited for another day.

CHAPTER 28

THE HEALING OF SIR URRÉ

THE aim of knighthood was for every man to lead the best possible life, following the teaching of Christ. For some men, like Sir Percivale, the life was of thought and inner spiritual struggles; for some, like Sir Bors and Sir Lancelot, it was of administration, government, and fighting; for some, like Taliessin, it was of poetry or learning. The important thing in any way of life was its purity, which meant the completeness with which it followed its aim, and the freedom of distraction from that aim. This purity, or concentration, has always been recognized as man's chief source of strength, under different names in each generation, but the same thing behind the names. King Arthur's knights regarded the keeping of their vows of knighthood as the source of their skill in battle, which was the reason why the good men always won and the traitors always lost. If it looks too simple to be true to us, we must beware lest we have lost the clarity of heart which sees the connection between right living and a happy daily life.

Sir Lancelot never regarded himself as one in close touch with God. He never saw the Holy Grail uncovered, and he worked no miracles. He was given the gift of victory and of excelling in arms, and he accepted that as his portion of good. He maintained love in courtesy in daily life towards every one, whether he felt it towards them or not, but it never occurred to him that this was in itself a miracle. He regarded himself as shut off from spiritual excellence by his failure in his vow of single devotion to the Queen because of his tricked marriage with Elaine and the birth of Galahad. He was to himself a lesser man than the youngest knight who with concentration of heart loved his lady and served God under the King.

But Sir Urré came seeking the best knight in the world, and inevitably Sir Lancelot was involved. Sir Urré was a knight of Hungary, a knight errant and of adventures, which meant that he was not in the service of any king but held his vows privately, and rode from one place to another seeking opportunities for a knightly life. When he was in Spain he fought a Spanish knight Sir Alpheus, and after being badly wounded he killed him. Sir Alpheus's mother was a witch, and in her grief for her son's death she put a spell on Sir Urré that his wounds should never heal unless the best knight in the world touched them.

So there Sir Urré lay helpless, with seven ghastly wounds that festered and bled, three in his head, three in his body, and one in his left hand, and his life drained away through them. In frantic haste his mother and sister arranged for a horse-litter, put him into it, and took horse themselves with a page to look after the animals, and set out on an almost hopeless search for the best knight in the world. No one knew if that meant the champion fighter, who of course was claimed by every city in turn throughout Europe, or the best spiritually, who might be completely obscure and only to be found by accident or by trying every knight in the world. But Sir Urré's mother had faith and therefore sense, and she began at the first place she came to and went straight on to the next, and so on through Europe.

The little party worked up from Spain, through Gaul and the land of the North Germans, the Danes, and into the kingdom of the Norsemen. They took ship and crossed to Orkney and down into Scotland. Sir Urré was growing very weak. In Scotland his mother heard that the King of Britain would hold his court at Carlisle, on the border between Scotland and Britain, at Pentecost in two weeks' time, and that there would be a great gathering of knights. So she set out for Carlisle.

When the court assembled she had an audience of King Arthur and told him her story. She told of all her travels and how many good knights had tried and failed to heal her son. King Arthur summoned all his knights. Sir Lancelot was out on a mission and would not be back till evening. To the rest King Arthur told the story of Urré, and announced that every knight should try in turn to heal him, and that to keep them from being too modest to try he himself would try first. Although he believed in his heart that Sir Lancelot was the best knight in the world, the King had learned that God's grace will strike anywhere, and must be expected everywhere. The unlooked-for distinctions of Sir Balin, Sir Galahad, Sir Percivale, and Arthur himself as an unknown lad of fifteen, had grounded him in this doctrine of equality.

So the long procession past the sick man began. Sir Urré was taken out of the litter and laid on rugs on the ground. A golden cushion was put beside him for each man to kneel on. King Arthur knelt first, and said: 'Sir, I am grieved for your hurt, and to encourage all other knights I will ask you to let me touch your wounds.' Sir Urré responded weakly, and the King touched him. But the wounds gaped unhealed. After King Arthur came the chief lords, or lesser kings, the King of Northumberland, King Anguish of Ireland, Carydos of Scotland, Constantine, son of Duke Cador of Cornwall, and the other rulers under King Arthur. The wounds remained unhealed.

Then the knights came forward, Gawaine, the King's nephew, first, and his three sons and four brothers, all the unreliable Orkney clan, and each one failed. Next came

See p. 212

Sir Lancelot passed through them from the realm of Britain

Sir Lancelot's family, ten of them, and they all failed. So it went on through the day. The names are listed by Sir Thomas Malory, to the number of one hundred and ten. The sick man was exhausted by the strain of hoping, and by the touch of all those hands. At last came news that Sir Lancelot's company had been seen and the King sent a message to him to attend the court at once. Sir Lancelot rode straight on to the field, and the heralds blew for his arrival. Both Sir Urré and his sister were stirred by a strange feeling as he dismounted, as though something profoundly important had happened.

But when the King told Sir Lancelot the story and eagerly would have led him to the sick man, the dark smiling face changed and the King realized that he had stumbled on something in his friend that he knew nothing about, and had hurt him badly. Lancelot was dismayed. To try to prove by working a miracle that he was the best knight in the world was against all his ideas, and, knowing his secret sins, he refused to attempt it. He did not explain his reasons to the King, because there were too many people listening, but he said that where so many kings and knights had failed it would be sinful conceit to try.

'You have no choice,' said the King, smiling, 'for I order you to do as we all have done.'

No one would have dared to refuse again. The great knight, the King's friend and the commander of his forces, hesitated, knowing it was mutiny in the face of all the gathered lords and knights. He drew a long breath and met the King's eyes, and refused. His eyes implored the King.

'My most renowned lord,' he said, 'I know well I dare not and may not disobey you. But I cannot take upon myself to touch that wounded knight with the intention of showing that I am better than all other knights. Jesu keep me from that shame.'

'Sir, you take it wrong,' said Arthur, answering the entreaty he felt as well as the words he heard. 'You will not be doing it for conceit, but to keep us company because you are a member of the Round Table. Therefore'—his voice was warm—'I pray you, do as we have done.'

Suddenly the wounded man raised a feeble and unexpected voice: 'Courteous knight, I entreat you for God's sake heal my wounds! Ever since you arrived it seems to me that they do not hurt so much as they did.'

'My lord,' said Sir Lancelot earnestly, 'Jesus grant that I could help you. I am bitterly ashamed to be thus tested, for never have I been able in worthiness to do so great a thing.'

Then he stepped forward, taking off his gauntlets, and said: 'My lord Arthur, I must obey your order, which is utterly against my wishes.' He knelt down, paused, and looked to the east and said quietly: 'Now blessed Father, Son, and Holy Ghost, I beseech Thee of Thy Mercy that my ordinary reputation may be saved, and, Blessed Trinity, Thou canst give me power to heal this sick man by Thine own great virtue and grace, but, good Lord, never by mine.'

Then he touched the wounds. The King, watching, drew a sharp breath, and stepped forward, peering. Suddenly he knelt down, his face amazed. Others moved forward, looked, and knelt. Sir Urré's wounds were closed, healed, and vanished. For a minute there was dead silence as those nearest knelt, and Sir Lancelot remained motionless. The King's voice was heard thanking God and His Blessed Mother. Then a cheer began to roll round the field. Sir Lancelot knelt, seeing and hearing nothing but the glory of the Trinity which had allowed him to work the miracle. People surged to and fro, shouting, laughing, and cheering, but Sir Lancelot still knelt, and the tears poured down his face.

CHAPTER 29

THE CIVIL WAR

IN spite of occasional great deeds by Sir Lancelot and the leaders, the Round Table was breaking down. An ideal of brotherhood and justice in Christ had been formed by King Arthur, and maintained for more than thirty years. Under its inspiration deeds had been done which had put Britain at the head of Christendom, deeds which were to fire men's imaginations through every century. But first the Hallows were misused, and withdrew, and then the whole effort faltered and failed through the clog and drag of sin. Yet to the end the glory of the Round Table was such that men remember its attempt rather than its failure, and in every generation wherever men are moved by high thoughts and deeds of love, brotherhood, and self-sacrifice, the life of King Arthur and the Round Table springs up again in their minds.

The final breakdown was caused by war between the King and Sir Lancelot. This tragedy was brought about by members of the Orkney clan, who nursed 'a great anger and unhappy that slackened not till the flower of chivalry of the world was destroyed and slain.' The Orkney clan were the sons of King Arthur's sister Morgause, Queen of Orkney, married to King Lot who had been killed. The head of it was Gawaine, and under him his brothers Gaheris, Agravaine, and Gareth, and Mordred, his half-brother, and all their sons and relations. They were mostly ambitious men, who wanted power rather than justice, and were jealous of any man greater than themselves, chiefly the King's right-hand man, Sir Lancelot.

To them he was a Frenchman from Bayonne who, by a hold on the Queen, had wormed his way into power and position which should be theirs. Next to Sir Lancelot the Orkney knights hated the Queen. By this time their hatred had become a settled policy, a determination to bring down Sir Lancelot and the Queen at any cost, by lies and malice if true opportunity did not arise. Only Gawaine and Gareth were exceptions.

Gawaine was the eldest; he had spent his early years with the golden youth of the Round Table, and though he was vain, worldly, and proud, he could not cut himself off entirely from the glories he had known. He had not spent thirty years with Lancelot's courtesy and King Arthur's steadfast goodness for nothing. Gareth was the youngest, and the poison of the clan had missed him.

But the rest of the clan were full of malice, in which the leaders were Agravaine and Mordred.

Now Sir Agravaine called a family council. He began by saying that Sir Lancelot was plotting to make himself king with the Queen's help, and that it was the clan's duty as relations of King Arthur to defend him.

The result was that Sir Mordred, Sir Agravaine, and twelve kindred knights of the Round Table caught Sir Lancelot unarmed in an ambush in the palace at Carlisle. He was alone with the Queen and had no armour on, and only his sword. The door was locked, and the fourteen stood in the passage outside. They called on him to come out as a traitor and be taken. Both Sir Lancelot and the Queen knew that if the Orkney knights dared to do this in the palace itself it was an open declaration of war. Sir Lancelot was desperately afraid for the Queen. If he were killed the traitor clan would have her burned alive.

'Now I would sooner have my armour on me than be lord of all Christendom,' he said.

They called on him to come out as a traitor and be taken

The enemy knights had carried a form from the hall and were preparing to break in the door. Lancelot called to them and said he was going to open. The Queen stood behind the door and Lancelot opened it a little. Sir Colegrevaunce rushed in and the Queen slammed the door and bolted it. Lancelot sprang in on Sir Colegrevaunce and with one blow of his bare fist broke his neck. He and the Queen got the armour off the dead man, and laced it on Sir Lancelot. Then the Queen hid and Sir Lancelot threw open the door. At the first stroke he killed Sir Agravaine, and one after another all the rest. But unfortunately, when Sir Agravaine fell, Sir Mordred fled, sure now of being sole leader of the clan. It was he who has the ill fame of bringing about the ruin of the kingdom.

Sir Lancelot stood breathing hard among the slain. Thirteen knights of the King's Round Table killed in his own palace! However true a friend he was, the King would have to punish Sir Lancelot for this. He left the Queen, who fully understood the seriousness of the situation, promising her his support in all dangers which might be coming, and went back to his own apartments. There he called an urgent council of his own clan, the men of Benwick and their followers. Ector, Bors, Lionel, Blamour, and many others, Lavaine of Astolat, and Urré of Hungary whom Sir Lancelot had healed, were all at court and attended the meeting. They heard the story and with one voice, uttered by Sir Bors, they answered:

'All is welcome that God sends us, and as we have received much good with you and much honour, we will take the ill with you as we have taken the good.' They all agreed too that he must stand by the Queen. Mischief was afoot, and they knew it would strike first at her.

'So, my fair lords, my kin, and my friends,' said Sir

Lancelot, knowing that it was possible that no less than civil war might break out, 'what will you do?'

'We will do as you will do,' replied Sir Bors.

Sir Lancelot outlined his plan and they discussed and filled in the details.

Meanwhile Sir Mordred and Sir Gawaine led their clan to demand an audience of the King. They told him that Sir Agravaine and twelve members of their family had caught Sir Lancelot plotting with the Queen, and had been killed for their pains. They demanded that the Queen should be burned and Sir Lancelot outlawed.

The King heard them out, with his heart breaking. The Orkney men had beaten him at last. For years they had been gnawing at the foundations of order, justice, and love, by indifference, violent angers, and slander. Now they had succeeded, and had brought down the King's work. They showed in themselves the baser elements in men which the life of knighthood had in other men held in place and ennobled. Now those elements, long encouraged secretly by this dark and violent family, rose up and by a trick overthrew that better life. The King knew that the Orkneys were too powerful to be ignored. Thirteen Round Table knights of their clan killed by Sir Lancelot had to be avenged, although the King did not doubt that Mordred had worked some trick. The triumph in his pale face convinced the King of it.

'In the name of God, make you ready,' the King said in a voice they had never heard, and gave orders for the arrest of the Queen.

The next morning, as Sir Lancelot expected, Sir Mordred carried out the first of his plans. The Queen was led out to be burned. The Benwick ambush was ready, and at the signal they fell upon the procession and escort. Hardly a man escaped the fury of Sir Lancelot and his companions.

This first engagement of the war which was to slay all the leaders of chivalry and honour was, with the last battle, the most bitter of all. Twenty-four knights were killed, including Sir Gaheris and Sir Gareth, who fell by Sir Lancelot's hand unknowingly in the hurly-burly. Again Sir Mordred had escaped, for he was not among the escort.

The Queen stood trembling in her condemned criminal's smock, where her jailers had left her when they fled. Sir Lancelot rode to her 'and made put a petticoat and a frock upon her, and then he made her to be set behind him and prayed her to be of good cheer.' The whole company rode off at top speed from Carlisle to Sir Lancelot's stronghold of Joyous Gard (which was either at Alnwick or Bamborough), and did not draw rein until they clattered into its safe keeping, and the portcullis clanged down behind the last man.

The country was in a ferment, every knight hastening to the nearest town or castle for news. The war began to take shape as men joined one side or the other. Every one feared and hated the Orkneys, and they did no good to the King's side. Yet the King held men's vows. The whole kingdom was split. A formidable gathering of northern lords and knights collected in and round Joyous Gard to fight on Sir Lancelot's side.

In the meantime the death of Gaheris and Gareth had turned Gawaine's last streak of goodness to bad. He took their deaths as personal spite of Sir Lancelot against two who had been his friends. From then on Sir Gawaine led even Sir Mordred in implacable hate. The preparations for war went on fast, and before summer was on the wane the King's host set out on the march to Joyous Gard.

They encamped round the wall of the town, inside which the mighty castle towered over the houses. Sir Lancelot was the finest soldier of his time, and he had not neglected his own stronghold.

The battle was fierce and noble knights on both sides fell. 'And ever was King Arthur about Sir Lancelot to have slain him, and ever Sir Lancelot suffered him and would not strike again. So Sir Bors encountered with King Arthur, and Sir Bors smote him, and so he alighted and drew his sword and said to Sir Lancelot, "Sir, shall I make an end of this war?" for he meant to have slain him. "Do not dare," said Sir Lancelot. "On pain of your head, touch him no more."' Then he got off his horse and raised the King and said to him:

'My lord the King, for the love of God end this strife. I pray you, remember what I have done in many places, and now I am evilly rewarded.'

The King looked on his lifelong friend and 'the tears broke out of his eyes, thinking of the great courtesy that was in Sir Lancelot more than in any other man. And therewith the King rode his way and could no longer look on him, saying to himself: "Alas, alas, that ever this war began."'

The battle went on for many days, breaking off with the fall of darkness and starting again in the morning. Sir Gawaine wounded Sir Bors very badly and was wounded himself, but no one succeeded in hurting Sir Lancelot. The King's forces made no headway at all.

While this unsatisfactory series of battles was going on, a stern command came to the King from the Pope. News of the civil war and the threat to Queen Guenevere had reached the Pope, who sent the Bishop of Rochester with a bull or sealed letter telling the King to remember his marriage vow and take his wife back again and make peace with Sir Lancelot. The King returned to Carlisle to receive the Pope's messenger. 'Full gladly he would have made peace with Sir Lancelot, but Sir Gawaine would not let him.' He threatened the King with civil war with the Orkneys if the King made peace with Sir Lancelot. They agreed, however, to take back the Queen. Safe conduct was granted to Sir Lancelot, and the Bishop took the message to Joyous Gard.

Sir Lancelot was suspicious that it was a trap by the Orkneys to get hold of the Queen, but the Bishop pledged his word and the Pope's order, and so Sir Lancelot let her go. He took a hundred knights, clothed in green velvet, their horses clothed in the same to the heels, every knight holding an olive branch. The Queen had twenty-four ladies following her dressed in the same way. Sir Lancelot was attended by twelve young nobles on chargers, dressed in white velvet with gold bands, with precious stones gleaming in their cloaks. Their horses' trappings were of white velvet. At their head rode the Queen and Sir Lancelot, both in cloth of gold.

Twenty-five years ago the young King had sent his friend Sir Lancelot to bring his bride Guenevere to Camelot, and they had come in the spring of youth and hope with ceremony and music to the King. Now that friend, veteran leader of the King's armies and outlaw in his realm, brought the Queen under clouds of anger and suspicion back to a ruined court. They had all passed their youth, and where achievement should have been growing under their feet, black loss and failure gaped. Yet as King Arthur and Sir Lancelot met in each other's presence for the last time, they knew that they were stronger than these men who had beaten them by malice and a trick. Beaten them? No, they were still what they had been, servants of Jesus Christ and brothers of the Round Table. They who had fought the twelve great battles which had broken the heathen, who had seen the Holy Grail and walked with angels, who had made Britain from end to end a land of peace and justice, could they be broken? Their work was ended, yes, for this century and place. It could never be ended while the power of God moved men's hearts. They were for ever greater than their enemies.

But at this moment they could do nothing. Sir Gawaine sat at the King's right hand, and the enemy filled every seat round him.

Sir Lancelot alighted and gave the Queen his hand. They came to the royal throne and knelt before the King. He sat silent. Sir Lancelot rose, raised the Queen, and said in a voice for all to hear:

'My most redoubted King, by the Pope's command and yours I have brought to you my lady the Queen, as is right. If there be any knight, of whatever rank, except yourself, who will dare to say that she is not wholly true to you, I here myself, Sir Lancelot du Lac, will prove upon his body that she is.'

Sir Gawaine sprang up and began wildly accusing him. He brought up the death of Gareth and Gaheris, and Sir Lancelot defended himself. He offered in penance to walk barefoot from Sandwich to Carlisle, and at every ten miles to found and equip a religious house, of any order the King chose, to say prayers for the souls of Gareth and Gaheris. Sir Gawaine clenched his fist and rejected the offer, and all terms of peace. He declared, while the King sat silent, that Sir Lancelot was exiled, and had fifteen days to leave the country, and that wherever he went Sir Gawaine would follow him till one or other was dead.

Lancelot looked at the King. He sat like stone. The Queen stood motionless. Seconds passed. All three knew that the old life was broken, and that an end had come. Patching up was useless. 'Then Sir Lancelot sighed, and the tears fell on his cheeks, and he said: "Most noble Christian realm, whom I have loved above all other realms! In thee have I won most of my honour, and now that I must depart in this manner, I regret that I ever came here, to be thus shamefully banished, undeserved and causelessly. In this realm I had honour, and by me and mine the Round Table was increased more in honour than ever it was by any one of you."' He returned Sir Gawaine's challenge and said he would answer his charge of treason wherever Sir Gawaine followed him. Then he turned to the Queen and there was silence in the hall.

'Madam, now I must leave you and this noble fellowship for ever. And since it is so, I beseech you to pray for me, and I will pray for you. If any false tongues accuse you, swiftly, my good lady, send me word; and if any knight's hand under heaven may deliver you by battle, I will deliver you.' Slowly he kissed her, and then gave her into the King's hand. He turned, and by an unbidden movement the whole hall stood to mark his going, as many times in the past these same men had stood to acclaim his victories. In silence, magnificent in cloth of gold, Sir Lancelot passed through them from the realm of Britain. 'And there was neither king, duke, earl, baron, nor knight, lady, nor gentlewoman, but all they wept as people out of mind, except Sir Gawaine.'

CHAPTER 30

THE DEPARTURE OF SIR LANCELOT

SIR LANCELOT called all his kinsfolk and friends together in the hall of Joyous Gard. He renamed the castle Dolorous Gard, and told them he was exiled and was going back to his lands in France, and asked what they would do. They all decided to go with him. 'For we all know that in this realm there will be no peace, but always quarrels and strife, now the fellowship of the Round Table is broken. For by the noble fellowship of the Round Table was King Arthur sustained, and by that nobleness the King and all the realm lived in peace and security. And a great part was because of your nobleness, Sir Lancelot.'

He offered each of them portions of the Benwick territories, for he was lord of great provinces in western and southern France. So they took ship at Cardiff and sailed to Benwick, which is thought to be Bayonne. There Sir Lancelot gave every man the lands he had promised. He himself set out to travel through all his territories to see their preparations for war and the readiness of the towns for siege. He knew that Sir Gawaine would come and he meant to be ready for him.

Sure enough, in a few months he received news that Sir Gawaine and King Arthur had sailed from Cardiff with an army. Sir Mordred had been left as governor of the kingdom and protector of the Queen. In a few weeks the British force was ravaging Sir Lancelot's lands. In Benwick Sir Lancelot held a council of war. Sir Bors urged open combat, Sir Lionel urged waiting until the enemy had run out of food and fuel and then to attack them. They all insisted that there was to be no more sparing of the King and showing of courtesy, as had been Sir Lancelot's rule in Britain. Here they were on their own ground and King Arthur had invaded them, and they wanted to be free to treat him as an enemy.

The result of the council was that an embassy of peace was sent by the hand of a damsel and a dwarf to the King's camp. But when she had delivered her message the King gave Sir Gawaine leave to answer her, and a defiant answer was returned and the offer of peace rejected.

Next morning Benwick was besieged. For six months the siege went on. Every day Sir Gawaine rode in front of the main gates and took on a knight in single combat, and he always won. There were skirmishes and jousts but no serious engagements, and the months dragged on. Then Sir Lancelot agreed to joust with Sir Gawaine, who had defeated and wounded so many of his leading knights. They met at last, and the battle was long and hard. For three hours, says Sir Thomas Malory, they fought, but in the end Sir Lancelot laid Sir Gawaine helpless on the ground. He drew back and left him. Sir Gawaine ground his teeth and shouted to him to finish him off, swearing that as soon as he was healed he would seek him out again. Sir Lancelot answered haughtily that he would be ready for him, but that nothing would induce him to kill a helpless man.

Sir Gawaine was carried to his tent and lay there for three weeks while his wound healed. When he was well he came out and challenged Sir Lancelot again. They fought again, and the result was the same. As Gawaine lay, frantic with defeat and helplessness, he still brandished his sword and tried to stab Sir Lancelot, shouting defiances at him.

Sir Lancelot turned away, saying: 'Whenever you can

stand on your feet, I will fight you, but I will not strike a wounded man who cannot stand.' He went back inside the city gates.

Sir Gawaine's madness refused to yield to any sense or persuasions from the King or his own friends. He did not care if the whole army perished of cold and hunger in the oncoming winter, so long as his thirst for vengeance was satisfied. The only plan he would listen to was to wait till his wound was healed and then to fight Sir Lancelot again.

But events were not left to the sole disposition of Sir Gawaine. When he was within three days of the next battle, there came news from Britain to King Arthur which brought the whole camp to its senses. Mordred had said that he had received news that the King and Sir Lancelot had been killed; he had therefore declared himself King, had been crowned, and was about to force the Queen to marry him. She had shut herself up in the Tower of London, and Mordred was laying siege to it. He had defied the Church and seized the government.

Gawaine and his grievances were forgotten. The King ordered his host to pack and take horse. The siege was raised, and the King made all speed to the coast to take ship for Britain.

CHAPTER 31

THE LAST BATTLE AND THE DEATH OF ARTHUR

SIR MORDRED was ready for the King's return. The moment he had planned so long had come. It was he of whom Merlin had said on the day when Arthur won his sword Excalibur that a son of Arthur's own sister would be the destruction of his kingdom. That prophecy was soon to be fulfilled.

News of the King's approach to Dover reached Mordred, and he prepared to resist him with a large force drawn up on the beach. 'Then there was launching of great boats and small, and full of noble men of arms; and there was much slaughter of gentle knights, and many a bold baron was laid full low, on both parties. But King Arthur was so courageous that no manner of knight could stop him landing, and his knights fiercely followed him. And so they landed in spite of Sir Mordred's host and all his power, and put Sir Mordred aback so that he fled and all his people.'

But in the landing Sir Gawaine, the leader of the feud against Sir Lancelot, was mortally wounded. Sir Lancelot was in France, but before he died Sir Gawaine made his peace with him, saying aloud to the King and all the knights gathered round: 'Through me and my pride you have all this shame and discomfort, for had that noble knight Sir Lancelot been with you, as he was and would have been, this unhappy war had never been begun; for he, through his noble knighthood and noble blood, held all your cankered

See p. 219

Mordred hurled himself forward to smite the king

enemies in subjection and danger.' He asked for paper, and wrote to Sir Lancelot, asking him to return to England to the help of the King, and to see his tomb and pray for his soul.

At noon he died, and the knights buried him in a chapel in Dover castle. There was now only Mordred left of the Orkney clan, King Arthur's own blood, which had destroyed his kingdom.

The next day there was another skirmish between the King's forces and Sir Mordred's, which ended in the withdrawal of the rebels. Then both sides collected their forces for a decisive blow. Mordred's stronghold was Canterbury. The King's strength lay in the west, so he set out to march in that direction, gathering forces as he went. Where the last battle was fought we do not know. It was on the coast, probably of Somerset, but in those days tidal sea-marshes covered half of what we know as Somerset, so that the site of the battle to-day is probably far inland, near Glastonbury, where Joseph of Arimathea landed on English soil with the Holy Grail which had caused all this strange history. We only know that it was somewhere on a far west sea coast and on a misty day.

On the night before the battle King Arthur had a dream. He dreamed that Sir Gawaine came to him and warned him that if he fought Sir Mordred on the next day he would be killed as well as the enemy. He must make a treaty postponing the battle for a month, and offer Mordred whatever terms would make him agree. In a month Sir Lancelot would arrive, and joining with the King would ensure the defeat of the rebels.

The King awoke and sent for his leaders and told them his dream. They all agreed to obey it. Sir Lucan and Sir Bedivere and two bishops were sent to Mordred's camp to offer terms. Finally Mordred agreed to make peace at the price of getting Cornwall and Kent immediately, and being made King Arthur's heir to the whole of Britain. A meeting was arranged to sign the treaty between King Arthur and Mordred, with fourteen attendants each, on the downland between their two armies. Neither side trusted the other, and each side was instructed by its leader to be fully armed, and if a single sword were drawn on the enemy side to rush into battle.

The King and Sir Mordred met, the treaty was signed, and wine was fetched to mark its signing. As they waited an adder came out of a bush and stung a knight in the foot. He seized his sword to kill the adder, and instantly both suspicious, watchful armies blew their trumpets and horns, drew swords, and rushed upon each other. 'And never since then was there seen a more doleful battle in any Christian land, for there was but rushing and riding, thrusting and striking, and many a grim word was there spoken, and many a deadly stroke.' To and fro surged the hosts, the rebels being slowly driven back but fighting every step, for they knew there would be no quarter. At last they broke back over a hillside and found themselves where

the long mountains ended in a waste
Of ever-shifting sand, and far away
The phantom circle of a moaning sea.
There the pursuer could pursue no more,
And he that fled no further fly the King;
And there, that day when the great light of heaven
Burn'd at his lowest in the rolling year,
On the waste land by the waste sea they closed.

The beach and mountains rang with the slaughter, the trumpets ordering the battle, the crash of the battle-axe, spear, and sword, the screams of horses, and the shouts of men. 'And thus they fought all the long day, and never slackened till the noble knights were laid to the cold earth. And ever they fought till it was near night, and by then was there a hundred thousand dead upon the earth.'

When the dolorous day
Grew drearier toward twilight falling, came
A bitter wind, clear from the North, and blew
The mist aside, and with that wind the tide
Rose, and the pale King glanced across the field
Of battle: but no man was moving there;
Nor any cry of Christian heard thereon
Nor yet of heathen; only the wan wave
Brake in among dead faces, to and fro
Swaying the helpless hands, and up and down
Trembling the hollow helmets of the fallen.

Of all that mighty host only two remained alive to stand beside the King, Sir Lucan and Sir Bedivere, and they were both wounded. 'Would to God,' said the King, glaring round on the dead and grasping his sword Excalibur, 'that I knew now where is that traitor Sir Mordred who has caused all this evil.' Then 'he was aware where stood Sir Mordred leaning upon his sword among a great heap of dead men.' Sir Lucan tried to restrain the King, reminding him of his dream, and how his life had been spared so far, and that the day was his since there were three of them left, and of the enemy only Sir Mordred lived. But the King was he who had fought twelve battles against the heathen and lived all his life in arms, and this moment, with all his knights dead about his feet, was not the time for him to flinch.

'Come death, come life,' he cried, 'now I see him yonder alone, he shall never escape my hand!' They ran at each other. The King's sword thrust right through Sir Mordred, who in his death agony hurled himself forward right against the hilt to smite the King on the helmet and pierce through his head. They both fell, Mordred dead and the King desperately wounded.

> Then, because his wound was deep,
> The bold Sir Bedivere uplifted him,
> And bore him to a chapel nigh the field,
> A broken chancel with a broken cross,
> That stood on a dark strait of barren land:
> On one side lay the Ocean, and on one
> Lay a great water, and the moon was full.

As they carried the King on that short journey, Sir Lucan died, and Sir Bedivere was left alone with the King and the dead. King Arthur felt his end was drawing near, and he remembered Excalibur, his sword. On one side of the blade was carved 'Take me,' and on the other 'Cast me away.' With the sword he had won and held the kingdom for Christ, and now the end was come.

He said to Sir Bedivere: 'Take my good sword Excalibur, and go with it to the water's edge and throw my sword into the water, and come again and tell me what you saw.'

Sir Bedivere took Excalibur and began to climb down to the shore. All the way down the magic and the worth of Excalibur worked in his mind, until, as all men had desired the Holy Grail, he desired to possess it for a purpose of his own and not to serve the purpose of the thing itself. He half desired it for its value and beauty in precious stones, and half as a relic of the King. On the seashore he held the long blade in his hands, and the moonlight turned the bloodstains black and ran like sparks round his hand,

> For all the haft twinkled with diamond sparks,
> Myriads of topaz lights, and jacinth work
> Of subtlest jewellery. He gazed so long
> That both his eyes were dazzled as he stood,
> This way and that dividing the swift mind,
> In act to throw.

He did not throw it. He hid Excalibur under a stunted tree, and went back to the King and told him he had done his bidding. Eagerly the King raised himself in his weakness. 'What did you see?'

'Sir, I saw nothing but water lapping and darkening waves.'

The King stared at him, and then realized the truth. 'You have lied to me,' he said. 'Now go quickly and do what I told you; as you are dear and precious to me, spare not, but throw it in.'

Sir Bedivere went again, but all the way he thought that the King was weak and dying, and did not know what he was saying, and that it would be good for posterity if the sword were preserved. All the knights were killed, the King was dying, there would be left of their greatness not one trace or proof. The sword must be saved. He hid Excalibur again, and went a second time to King Arthur in the ruined chapel.

'What did you see?'

> And answer made the bold Sir Bedivere,
> 'I heard the water lapping on the crag,
> And the long ripple washing in the reeds.'

Then the King half rose in majesty and wrath, and that fire which had awed the heathen in battle and the faithless in his court flashed in its former power from his eyes. 'Ah, traitor and untrue, now you have betrayed me twice.'

Sir Bedivere shrank back.

'Who would have thought that you who have been so dear and precious to me, and called a noble knight, that you would betray me for the riches of this sword? But now go again quickly; for your long delay has put me in danger of my life, for I have taken cold. Unless you do as I tell you now, if ever I see you again I shall kill you with my own hands, for you would let me die for the sake of my rich sword.'

Sir Bedivere turned and fled. He ran down the rocky path and stumbled over the stones to the tree, seized Excalibur, and hurled it far out over the water.

> But ere he dipt the surface, rose an arm
> Clothed in white samite, mystic, wonderful,
> And caught him by the hilt, and brandished him
> Three times, and drew him under in the mere.

The knight's hair rose upon his head. King Arthur heard his steps running and slipping on the path, and knew before he spoke that he had been faithful the third time.

'Alas, help me hence,' said the King, 'for I am afraid I have stayed too long.'

Sir Bedivere lifted the King on his shoulders and carried him down to the water. There they found a barge hung with black from bow to stern, crowded with figures draped and veiled in black, and among them a crowned Queen with two other queens, all three veiled in black. From the barge rose a cry of lamentation as they approached, a mourning shriek and moan.

'Now put me into the barge,' said the King.

Sir Bedivere did so and the mourning figures received him and laid him down with his head in the Queen's lap.

As she took him she said: 'Ah, my dear brother! Why have you stayed so long from me?'

> And loosed the shatter'd casque, and chafed his hands,
> And called him by his name, complaining loud,
> And dropping bitter tears against a brow
> Striped with dark blood.

The barge began to draw away from the shore, and Sir Bedivere realized that he was left alone, and behind him lay a hundred thousand dead. 'My lord Arthur,' he cried, 'what will become of me, now you are going from me and leave me here alone?

'Now the whole Round Table is dissolved
Which was an image of the mighty world,
And I, the last, go forth companionless
And the days darken round me, and the years
Among new men, strange faces, other minds.'

'Comfort yourself,' answered the King from the barge, 'and do as well as you can, for I can do no more good for you. I must go into the vale of Avilion to heal me of my grievous wound.' The barge was moving away and his voice came faintly on the night air. 'If you never hear of me again, pray for my soul.'

Long stood Sir Bedivere,
Revolving many memories, till the hull
Look'd one black dot against the verge of dawn,
And on the mere the wailing died away.

Then he left the shore and climbed back on to the cliffs, and turning away from the battle-ground walked all night through the woods. In the early light he came to a chapel, and there he saw a hermit prostrate on the ground in prayer beside a new grave.

'Sir,' said Sir Bedivere, 'what man is buried here that you pray for so intently?'

'Fair son,' answered the hermit, 'I only know by guessing. This very night, at midnight, came a number of ladies who brought a dead man and prayed me to bury him.'

'Alas,' said Sir Bedivere, 'that was my lord King Arthur, who lies buried in this chapel.' He fainted as he spoke. When he recovered he asked the hermit if he might stay there always and serve him and pray for the soul of the King.

Long stood Sir Bedivere

But yet neither knew for certain what man lay buried there, nor where the barge had gone and the many ladies and the three queens. No man had known the secret of King Arthur's birth, and no man knew the secret of his end. The King said he was going to the vale of Avilion to be healed of his wound. And after he was healed? In the dark days of war and murder, robbery and burning, which came upon the land when Arthur's rule was gone, it was whispered that the King was not dead, that he had only been taken by the Lord into another place, and he would come again and free the land from tyranny and set up again the rule of justice and right. Men said that in an unknown tomb in a chapel in the wilds near Glastonbury there was carved in uncouth letters, scarcely readable:

HIC JACET ARTHURUS,
REX QUONDAM REXQUE FUTURUS

(Here lies Arthur, King that was and King that shall be.)

CHAPTER 32

THE DEATH OF GUENEVERE AND OF SIR LANCELOT

THE last battle had been fought, and all the ruling knights and lords of Britain had been killed, the King had vanished on his unknown destiny, and Britain had no ruler, no court, and no government. What of the Queen? She had shut herself in the Tower of London to resist Sir Mordred's intention of marrying her. There she stayed until the news came of the last battle, the death of all the knights, and the departure of the King. Then she put off her royal state, and dressed in black, and with five ladies took horse early one morning before any one was in the streets, and slipped out of London at the moment the gates were opened. Disguised as nuns they fled across Britain to the west, to Amesbury in Wiltshire, where there was an abbey, monastery, and nunnery.

The Queen became a nun, and put on the black-and-white habit, and led the strictest life in the convent. She showed such constancy and goodness, combined with the strength of her character, and knowledge of how to rule, that in time she was chosen Abbess and made head of the convent. There she stayed until the end of her life. But though her outward life had come to this harbour, there was one more incident awaiting her from the stormy world outside.

Sir Lancelot received the letter written by Sir Gawaine on his deathbed, telling him of Mordred's treachery, and asking him at once to come to the help of the King and the rescue of the Queen, and to pray for Gawaine's soul at his tomb. He did not know about the last battle. He and Sir Bors at once marshalled the fighting force of their family from all over France and came with speed to Britain. They landed at Dover, and were told of the news of the last battle and the collapse of the kingdom.

Before he did anything else, on hearing the news, Sir Lancelot made his peace with the dead Gawaine. He knelt for long hours by his tomb in the castle, and prayed for his soul. He gave alms of meat and fish, wine and ale, and twelve pence to every man and woman from the town and countryside, and himself gave each one the money, wearing a mourning gown. Lastly he gathered all the priests that could be found and had prayers said for the soul of Sir Gawaine, and gave one hundred pounds for these prayers to be continued.

With that the feud was healed, and Sir Lancelot turned to his next duty. He summoned all his followers and told them that he was going to look for the Queen. If he did not return in fifteen days they were to go home and he thanked them for their support. Sir Bors came to him after the council and urged him to take a few friends with him, as Britain was fast becoming a dangerous country again with bandits on the roads. But Sir Lancelot was thinking of other things and answered: 'Stay here, for I shall go on my journey, and neither man nor child shall go with me.'

His heart guessed where the Queen would have hidden, and he rode straight there. He knocked at the gate, and though no man was allowed within the nunnery, when the porter nuns saw the dark face of Sir Lancelot, known throughout Christendom, they backed away from the gate and left it open. In he walked, and passed unchallenged through courtyard after courtyard, the nuns gasping at the sight of him, and silently gliding away. He asked one where to find the Queen, and she pointed without speaking. He came round a corner, and saw her and stood still.

Then 'Queen Guenevere was aware of Sir Lancelot as she walked in the cloister. And when she saw him there she fainted three times.' Her nuns brought a seat, and Sir Lancelot stood still, waiting. When the Queen could speak, the nuns brought him to her. She said to them all and to him: 'Through this man and me has all this war happened, and the deaths of the noblest knights of the world, and through us is my most noble lord slain. Therefore, Sir Lancelot, you must know that I am in great difficulty to get my soul healed. And therefore, Sir Lancelot, I demand, and implore you, for the sake of all the love that was between us, that you never see me face to face again. For God's sake, never come near me again. Go back to your kingdom, and keep it well from war and harm, for well as I have loved you in the past, my heart can no longer bear the strain of seeing you. And I pray you, pray for me.'

'Now, my beloved,' said Sir Lancelot, 'do you want me to go away to my country? That I will never do, for I shall never betray all the promises I have made to you. But the same life you have taken to, I will take to, for the love of Jesus, and to pray especially for you.'

'Ah, Sir Lancelot, if you would do it, and keep to it!' said the Queen.

'Madam, never yet did you know me break my promise. Therefore, lady, since you have betaken yourself to perfection, I must also take myself to perfection, as is only right. For I witness before God, in you I have had my earthly joy, and if I had found you so disposed I had thought of taking you back to my own kingdom. But since I find you have chosen this life, I will betake me to penance and pray as long as I live. So, madam, I pray you, kiss me, and never again.'

'No, I will never do that,' said the Queen, and so they parted.

Sir Lancelot rode all day and all night, until he heard a bell ringing in the forest. He followed it and found the chapel where Sir Bedivere lived with the hermit, and from there he went no further, but stayed and became a hermit with them.

Meantime at Dover his friends were growing anxious. Sir Lionel rode to London to look for him, and was killed by bandits on the road. Sir Bors decided to send the host home, and then he, with Sir Lancelot's brother, Sir Ector, and a few of his closest friends, set out in search. They split into two parties under Sir Ector and Sir Bors. Sir Bors's party were led by the grace of God to the very hermitage where Sir Lancelot was. The service of the Eucharist was beginning as they tied their horses to a tree, and through the chapel door they saw the scarred face of Sir Lancelot above the hermit's dress. They slipped silently into the chapel and shared the service with Sir Lancelot, Sir Bedivere, and the other hermit. Afterwards they clasped hands, smiling, and there they stayed and lived a holy life with the others.

Within six months they were joined by more of the searching knights. 'When they saw Sir Lancelot had taken him to such perfection they had no wish to depart, but took the same life as he had.' For six years they lived so, and then Sir Lancelot became a priest.

It was soon after this that a vision came to him in the night that he was to take a horse-bier and go to Amesbury and there would find the Queen dead, and that he was to bury her beside King Arthur. Three times in the night the vision came, and in the morning Sir Lancelot got ready.

He and the seven friends with him walked from Glastonbury to Amesbury, and when they arrived at the nunnery they found that the Queen had died half an hour before they came. So with every pomp and care, with a hundred torches burning round the bier, they escorted the Queen for the last time, on the journey to Glastonbury.

After she was laid in the earth Sir Lancelot did not live more than six weeks. Neither food nor drink interested him, and although the loving Sir Bors and all his friends tended him he faded before their eyes. He scarcely slept at all, and was generally found contemplating the tomb of the Queen, cheerful but not interested in living. Soon he was too weak to get up from bed, and he made Sir Bors promise to take him all the way north to his own stronghold Joyous Gard and bury him there.

One night his friends woke suddenly, and by a common impulse went to Sir Lancelot's cell. They found him dead, and smiling, and the cell full of the most exquisite smell which had only come to them in the presence of the Holy Grail. After due ceremonies, they laid him in a horse-bier, and made the long journey to Joyous Gard. Arrived there, they laid his body in the choir of the castle chapel, and had services over it day and night for fifteen days, with candles burning day and night.

It was during this fortnight that Sir Ector found himself at Joyous Gard. Seeing the lights in the choir and figures moving he went in, and there he saw the dead body of his brother that he had sought so long.

'Ah, Lancelot!' he said. 'You were the head of all Christian knights. You were never matched by any earthly knight's hand. You were the most courteous knight that ever bore shield! You were the truest friend to your lover that ever bestrode a horse, and you were the truest lover among sinful men that ever loved a woman,

There he saw the dead body of his brother

and you were the kindest man that ever struck with a sword. You were the goodliest person that ever came among a company of knights, and you were the simplest and gentlest man that ever ate in hall among ladies, and you were the sternest knight to your mortal foe that ever put spear in rest.'

After the burial of Sir Lancelot the knights split up. Sir Bedivere stayed in the hermitage for the rest of his life, but the rest, with Sir Bors, went home to France to their own lands. From there they went on crusades to the Holy Land, where in the end they were killed fighting against the Turks, 'upon a Good Friday for God's sake.'